THE
CREATIVE
FORMULA

Compose, Choreograph, and
Capture Your Masterpiece

HOLLY SHAW

The Creative Formula: Compose, Choreograph, and Capture Your Masterpiece

For permission requests, please contact: hollyshawproductions@gmail.com

ISBN-13: 978-1536800050
ISBN-10: 1536800058

Written by Holly Shaw
Content editing by Norah Sarsour
Manuscript editing by Harlow Carpenter
Author photos by Aaron Fagerstrom
Cover Art and Formatting by Heidi Sutherlin

Published in the United States by:
Performers & Creators Lab
www.performersandcreatorslab.com

Printed in the United States of America

The Five-Part Study of One Gem exercise is influenced by Daria Halprin's communication feedback model and is used with written permission.

CONTENTS

DEDICATION

This book is dedicated to my little pink tornado.

ASK A MOTHER
HOW TO GET IT DONE

Ever since I could remember, I have always loved to perform and create. When I was very young, I would roller-skate around my garage. In the morning when other kids were still groggy, I was making up dances and singing show tunes at the end of my driveway, waiting for the school bus to arrive. Whenever I danced, whenever I was in front of people, I felt a palpable bright energy flowing out of me and toward them. I didn't really know what that was all about, but I knew that it made me hungry for more of it. I was a badly dressed little country bumpkin from Indiana, but *I had dreams*! I wanted to be a movie star! I convinced my dad to take me to Chicago, the biggest city nearby, and we walked the entire city for two weeks knocking on casting agents' doors until I found representation. I had my own agent by the time I was twelve. By the time I was sixteen, I was starring in a film on TV. At twenty-three, I was dancing on stages all over the world.

But there is nothing that can prepare you for being a parent, though being a parent will prepare you for everything else. When I became a single mother at the age of twenty-six, it was a shock to the system. My son was a needy pink tornado that came barreling through my life and left me to figure out how to put my house back together. Up until that point, my life's tune had been all about me. I'm no stranger to challenges, but becoming a single mom was

1

another thing entirely! When my son was born, my heart grew two million sizes bigger and lived outside of me in the form of this fragile, squalling bundle. I got super clear about what it was I wanted to be doing. There was room for what I loved: my kid and dance and a small, solid community of friends.

As I spent my days with my newborn son in my arms, I wondered to myself—with complete contempt—what the hell had I been doing with my life up to this point. Why did I waste so much of that glorious free time I used to have worrying about nonsense instead of making more art? The ambition wasn't gone, but any squandering of my time went out the window. They are our best teachers, these kiddos.

I used to work for an attorney who said that mothers make the best employees because they work like they need the money. I'd like to think that this is true, that we mothers do make the best employees, but I think it goes even further than our work ethic (and our need for money).

I think we mothers are some of the best creative thinkers because we are experts at time management, multitasking, problem solving, resourcefulness, keeping our cool, and soothing tense situations. Not to leave men or women without kids out of the equation. Sorry, guys—I love you, I do, and I know there are a lot of great creators who aren't moms. But juggle a crying baby on one arm while trying to adjust your shirt for breastfeeding, fold up a stroller, and explain to the bus driver that you'll just be a minute with fishing out that bus fare, and you'll understand what I'm talking about. And if we manage to do all of that and be good employees too, well, then congratulations on hiring us!

When I became a mom, my tolerance for bullshit-that-I-did-not-want-to-be-doing shrank, and I became an expert problem solver! How would I be able to take that amazing opportunity dancing for the Pacific Symphony? OK, hmm...an entire week away from home. Phone calls would be made, emails sent, scrambling, waiting, calling in favors, setting up the calendar, filling in any gaps...by the time I left for that gig, there was a master contact list, everyone knew who was handing my son off to whom, and my kid was actually excited about his week of sleepovers. I'd go to perform for a week, come back, and then the next week it would start all over again.

By thirty, I was producing my own shows. My son performed onstage in one of my shows at age six. I had my choreography commissioned or funded by the West Wave Festival, the Edinburgh Arts Festival, and the Hewlett Foundation for the Arts. I founded a nonprofit called the Eve's Elixir project, which provided a platform for artists of contemporary world dance wanting to take new risks. I was educating myself as a teacher and a director by studying the Life/Art Process at the Tamalpa Institute; studying with Andrew Wood of the Andrew Wood Acting School; studying contemporary dance with Benjamin Levy, among others; and exploring the world of hypnotherapy.

I'm not afraid to tell you that becoming a mother turned me into one of the most resourceful, creative, badass bitches I know. But the Creative Formula wouldn't come until years later...

MY YEAR OF MAKING 365 DANCES IN 365 DAYS

I was surviving—sort of. But I still didn't feel like much changed from year to year and felt this lump in my throat every time I saw some really great dance performance. I knew I wasn't done yet, yet it felt hard to do it all. As much as I tried to make it all work, I was still pretty limited compared to other artists I knew who were traveling the world with their dance companies and bands. I felt sad about my life and at times a little sorry for myself. It was an indulgent pity party. I knew it and didn't care. I saw myself just growing older and taking the route so many other dancers do, fading into retirement before they ever really make great work.

But then, about five years ago, I went through a deep change after being inspired by the movie *Julie & Julia*, in which the main character makes all the recipes in Julia Child's cookbook within one year. At the time, I was feeling stuck in my life. I was working full-time as an accountant, being a single mom, and trying to maintain my career as a dancer, while still trying to find time to make my own choreography. I was haunted by dreams of the work I wanted to be doing. I could envision it so clearly, but didn't see anyone anywhere doing it. I knew it was mine to make.

Well, after watching that movie, I thought, "You know, if I'm really serious about making dance, then why am I not making it? What's my big excuse? Don't I have ten minutes a day? Twenty?"

I decided—no more excuses. I challenged myself to create 365 dances in one year. To make a dance every single day, no matter whether I felt like it or not.

So I did just that.

This year of 365 dances changed my life more than I would realize at the time. At the end of it, I was laid off from my job, and my real life started. It was a life of not only making my own work, but helping others to create original work as well.

I learned so much in that year of personal study. I had to face my own fears, insecurities, feelings of inertia, depression, and the classic "What am I thinking? Who even cares?"

Pretty quickly I discovered that just showing up in the studio wasn't enough. I could easily kill the time thinking about what I might do, idly doing a few movements of dances I'd done before, or just "stretching" on the floor and trying to find the right music. Before I knew it, my time was up and I had to go onto my next obligation. I had to go to the grocery store, pick up my kid, run an errand—I was a single mom with a full-time job, and I only had a handful of hours each week to do this dance-making stuff. I couldn't screw around. My hard-earned money was paying for me to be an artist in the studio, and I had better figure out how to do it a hell of a lot better!

This is where the Creative Formula began: out of the need for efficiency.

At the time, I was also reading *Ask and It Is Given* by Abraham-Hicks and immersing myself in the study of their videos and materials about the Law of Attraction. I learned that the Law of Attraction was best utilized by tuning into your thoughts and feelings, and that you weren't just attracting things, but thoughts and creative inspiration as well. I began experimenting with this and noticing things:

I couldn't just plop myself into a studio and expect to work as well as I could if I had thought about what I wanted to do there beforehand.

Going into my studio to create dance worked best if I went there directly after a technique class.

I realized that attitude, mind-set, and the way that I felt amounted to everything when it came to doing great work, and that, blessedly, I had control over it! I experimented with that control and would test it even on my worst days. Could I go into the studio after, say, a bad fight with my boyfriend and step into my feelings rather than denying them? Could I still align with myself and mine the gold of that experience, alchemizing it into creative work?

And so I began to observe myself like I was Sherlock Holmes. If I had a good day in the studio where the ideas were flying, and I left with something I was actually kind of proud of, then I'd ask myself with deep curiosity:

What did I do that was different?

How was I able to generate all those cool moves and crank out phrases at top speed with very little effort?

I also assessed the other days when no amount of warming up or technique exercise could jump-start my imagination—those days when I just wanted to lie on the floor and cry.

When I would lie on the floor and cry, what was the matter then?

How did I get there?

What was going on that had led me to that place?

And how could I avoid it in the future?

As I answered these questions, the Creative Formula began to click into place. I saw with more clarity how to set up the most satisfying creative sessions where I could generate the good nuggets. I didn't fully stop having some bad days now and then, but when I did, I was able to retrace my steps and realize exactly where I had diverted my course. I was tuning in to the well of creativity and learning how to clear out the chatter so I could hear it better and better. I couldn't count on each day working in the studio being brilliant, but I could become a better listener.

THE BEGINNING OF THE PERFORMERS & CREATORS LAB

As I figured this out, it began to show in my work and performances. The work I was doing was different—not altogether great 100 percent of the time, but unique and spirited. I caught the attention of my peers, who would stare in disbelief at my sometimes-wildly-different-but-kinda-cool choreography. They started asking about it, and so I started sharing my secrets with my friends who were choreographers. Gradually they began offering to pay me to help them.

This was the time when I really started to imagine myself doing this seriously as a career. I wanted to lean into this work and make a special place for it: a place where that creative play could be taken seriously—as oxymoronic as that sounds. It was important to me that the work I was doing on my own and with others be given the room for experimentation, testing, formulating, re-trying. The word *laboratory* had just the right weight to it, and thus the Performers & Creators Lab was born. It is the name of my business, spacious enough to grow beyond myself. It exists in my in-home studio, in theaters that host me, and sometimes virtual online workshops where information can be shared, experiments can be run, and I can invite other artists to dare to explore. In the early years, it existed mainly in the little studio I was renting at the time, which sat behind a martial arts academy.

Here's how I began working with clients. A choreographer friend might call me and ask me to help them out with a piece. They were stuck on how to handle a commissioned piece, or they needed help figuring out a resolution to a number. We'd grab a coffee at Arizmendi on Lakeshore Avenue in Oakland, then head into the lab. We'd get to work. We'd listen to the music, they'd show me what they had so far, and I'd start asking questions: "How do you want this to feel?" "How do you feel doing it?" "I'm curious about this choice here at the end of this phrase. Was that abrupt transition intentional?"

Sometimes I'd give suggestions, but I realized that the more general my suggestions were, the better. "It'd be kinda cool if the piece took up more space at some point. How would that feel?" "You move a lot in a circular way. I wonder if it might be interesting to break it up with an abrupt linear movement forward during the final movement." The best work and ideas were to come from those general suggestions, and I knew it. My job was noticing things they might have missed, but more importantly, egging them on, getting them in touch with that part of them that knew what to do and was excited to get to work. I kept the Creative Formula in my mind the entire time, noticing when they were working against themselves by trying to articulate or figure it out when they weren't even in the mood. I knew from my own experience that I had to ease them into the whole thing and get them excited about the project before we ever began problem solving.

THE DEEPER LAB FLAMENCO DANCE INTENSIVE

Sharing these newfound creative tools was awesome, but the work really started to show some serious teeth when I started using it in the Deeper Lab Flamenco Dance Intensive. This is when the work moved from "something to help people be more creative" to "something to help people unlock their darkest shit, transcend it, and come barreling full force out the other side!" The testimonials to how the Creative Formula had helped people started pouring in after the first Deeper Lab:

> *"The workshop was just so profound. I didn't go into the weekend expecting it to be emotional, or expecting to feel so different afterward.*

I feel realigned internally."

These workshops were geared toward helping flamenco dance students push through their own barriers and go from learning flamenco to actually performing it, or even just feeling more comfortable and free in it. As a flamenco dancer myself who had struggled with this, it had always been a dream of mine to provide a creative space for flamenco dancers. In facilitating the Deeper Lab, I found that by using the energy of the group and guiding them with the tools of the Creative Formula, not only were they able to be more creative, but they were also busting through deep, unconscious, limiting beliefs about themselves.

"The biggest revelation was that inspiration can be scheduled. I don't have to wait for inspiration to find me."

Dancers reported having new experiences in their everyday lives that were richer, more honest. And things like stage fright that had plagued some of them for years would often vanish after working with the Creative Formula.

"Why I dance, where I am scared, where I want to go with it. I not only got to answer those questions, but I made a huge leap in facing the fears I have around dancing. And it was fun to face those fears! I left the workshop feeling like my relationship to flamenco and to my own artistry, is more in my own hands than ever before."

Meanwhile, my work helping out my peers in the studio grew organically and continued to blossom by word of mouth. Eventually, I began helping composers, singer-songwriters, actors, and even directors with their work. At the time of writing this book, I have now helped hundreds of performing artists to totally kill it onstage and create original work without feeling like they're selling out or losing their sanity. I lead group programs for artists all over the nation, both online and in the San Francisco Bay Area, through the Performers & Creators Lab. I also give talks on the topic of creativity and performance for different groups and universities.

The Creative Formula has helped to shape all of that. To this day, it serves as the core of all that I do, whether it's coaching onstage performances, facilitating creative masterminds, or teaching my signature flamenco workshop, the Deeper Lab Flamenco Intensive. The Creative Formula, with its emotional indicators, creates a road map for the creative process, helps me to unstick creatives, and, best of all, helps creatives learn how to unstick themselves.

"I feel like I have the tools now to get myself more aligned and start creating, which was my most pressing struggle."

This book is a map of the entire creative process from start to finish. In three simple steps, you'll understand how we go from a problem to a solution, from an empty studio to a finished piece. It is a way of understanding how the creative mind unfolds itself and deals with all of the problems along the way, like getting stuck, or feeling overwhelmed or jealous. The Creative Formula deals with that sometimes slippery skill of how to actually generate and complete an entire work.

THE MYTH OF THE ELUSIVE MUSE

Artists make work. That's one thing we know for sure! They create, put things together, and make stuff happen. They basically pull something out of their minds—out of the ether and into the present time. Their ideas become actual physical manifestations that other people can see, taste, touch, hear, and smell. If you are an artist, then creating stuff is your job. And if you're an artist, a creator, and you aren't making work, then you aren't getting any better at it! That's why when you are stuck, it can feel like such a nasty thing. You understand that you are no closer to creating a masterpiece than you are to the moon. And there is a part of you that isn't moving with the creative flow, which feels the worst of all. It happens to all of us at some point or another—we stop flowing down the river of creativity and get stuck in the brambles and mud on the shore.

But how would it feel to have a creative formula that served as a barometer to know when you're working for or against yourself in the studio? How would it feel to have an internal GPS system that was so strong, you would never doubt your own choices ever again? Imagine getting offstage and feeling great about it and thinking, "That was so much fun! What's next?"

The good news is that all of this is possible.

There are effective ways of easing the negativity in your head, the chatter of things like "Ugh! I always do this! Who am I to attempt this? This isn't even any good!" so you can get down to business and actually do the creative work. You can work with your zany creative brain to get started, keep going, and not only complete work that you love, but enjoy the process of creating!

There is a prevailing myth that a muse, a source of inspiration, is elusive and difficult to come by—it's something you have to catch, or else it will visit you only if and when you are lucky or very talented. I'd like to deal with this myth right away.

> The truth of the matter is this: artistic
> inspiration is available to us at all times.

Why is it, you ask, that I can't always seem to access it? Why is it that sometimes I find myself struggling in the mires of hard work, plodding along, trying to string together ideas piece by piece without much success? And why is it that at other times a good idea just falls right into my lap with a loud *plonk*, fully formed and lighting up with phenomenal energy? I can answer that one as well:

> It's not that your muse is elusive. It's that you're not letting it in.

Elizabeth Gilbert gave a TED talk called "Your Elusive Creative Genius," in which she asks us to consider that our muses exist outside of us, and that these muses show up at their own whim when they feel like it. While I understand the desire to assign our inspiration to something outside of ourselves, I would argue that assuming we have no control over when it shows up assigns responsibility in places that cannot really be controlled or influenced. It's true that sometimes we are inspired, and sometimes we aren't. Sometimes we sit down to write, or we go into the studio and create with fervor, and other times we do the thing, but the results are limp—it's true. Consistency is hard to come by with creativity. Showing up isn't a guarantee of engaging your muse—not because your muse has moved on to someone else, but because you aren't tuning into it. You can be working for hours and still not hear it. The Creative Formula isn't about making your muse show up. It's about making you a better listener.

In this book, I'll explain the three major ingredients of the Creative Formula and give you tools to make them work in unison. The Creative Formula explained in this way will demystify your art-making process so that the *doing* is not the mystery. Rather, you can focus on *exploring* your subject. It takes a lot of practice to make a masterpiece, so you don't want to be stuck in the figuring-out stage of the creative process. You need to have that part in the bag and find the enjoyment in *what* you are making, not *how*.

There are a bazillion books out there right now on the topic of creativity, and I can tell you why I think that is. We are at a time of great diversity on the planet. People have never been richer and happier and also have never treated each other so horribly in such massive numbers. Everything has become bigger and more. In this time of all kinds of disparity of wealth and experience, we are looking to creativity to give us new solutions to our problems. That's why the people I love helping are creators and performers— those of us tasked with the creating of stuff and imagining new ways of being. For me, this is the highest level of being a visionary. It's an important job, because if we can't imagine something different, than who else will?

So that's my theory of this creativity boom and the plethora of new books that have come of it. There are some great books out there, but they present mostly Band-Aid solutions without ever really dealing with the core of the creative process and flow—the mental and emotional process of how we really create stuff.

How many books on creativity do you have to flip through to make you more creative? Zero. You were born to create. Even if you don't create on purpose, you are still creating your life every day, moment to moment, by default. The Creative Formula is a road map that will help you out in the dark-night-of-the-soul moments. It will make your creative life not just easier, but more transparent and manageable.

Don't wait to read this book! If you have an idea for something, and you aren't taking action, then the light is dimming on it already. The moment you let an idea pass without taking it seriously, it will flip its hair and sashay away from you like a sexy girl ignored. Pay attention. Your future creative wifey is calling.

The information in this book could have you working on your next big piece by nightfall. By the end of the week, you will no longer feel stuck in a nightmare in your creative life. You won't be stubbing your toes on the rocky paths that aren't working for you. This book will hold your hand in the dark tunnel and show you the way out.

The Creative Formula is for people who are accountable to their relationship with their muse. It's for people who know they need to spend time with it and learn to listen to it. Like any good, mature relationship, your muse needs to know you are listening before it feels comfortable speaking its truth, getting intimate, and sharing the real golden moments with you. When you point your finger at your muse and say, "You're being elusive!" it will point right back and tell you, like any spiritually evolved partner would, "You're projecting!" There is no hiding from the truth of it. Either you're listening or you're not. This book gives you the tools to listen better.

Warning: Once you read this book, you'll know too much. You can never go back to claiming you are "overwhelmed" or "stuck." But I promise you won't want to anyway. You'll be too busy making work. Are you ready to begin?

HOW TO USE THIS BOOK

This is a straightforward book about creating for people
who would rather create than read a book about creating.

I'm a theatre and performance nerd, a creativity researcher, and a total transformation junkie. I can spend hours in a studio all by myself observing the effects of movement on my consciousness without being on any drugs whatsoever. It's endlessly fascinating to me! I've spent years reading books on composition, choreography, acting, directing, philosophy, performance psychology, and art therapy in an attempt to discern the real jewels in the art of making magic onstage. Most of those books aren't bestsellers, and they can be hard to get through because they're written by real academics. You may have to read a paragraph several times to understand what it's even saying, let alone comprehend how to turn theory into action. I didn't want my book to be like that. Having escaped the grad school experience, I also escaped the responsibility of writing like that. *The Creative Formula* is designed to be accessible, but also full of real artistic nuts and bolts. It's playful, but deadly serious.

DEFINITIONS AND THINGS YOU CAN DO

These first few chapters are designed to not only introduce you to the three main ingredients of the Creative Formula, but to serve as touchstones you can return to later. Each of the three ingredients, Alignment, Allowing, and Articulation, begins with a definition and a list of things you can do to evoke that step of the Creative Formula. These are for quick reference whenever you are stuck in a certain part of your creative process.

THE CREATIVE FORMULA IN ACTION

In addition to describing the three main ingredients of the Creative Formula, I've provided direct examples, exercises, and powerful tools. I've also included further insight into exactly how to put the Creative Formula into action in the chapters "The Creative Formula in the Studio," "The Creative Formula in Coaching Sessions," "The Creative Formula in the Classroom, Groups, or Workshops," and "The Creative Formula Onstage."

SELF-ASSESSMENT QUESTIONS

An important part of learning how the Creative Formula works and putting it into action is being able to clearly self-assess where you are at any moment. At the end of each of the chapters there are self-assessment questions you can ask that will help you sense whether you have worked each step enough to move on to the next. Your self-assessment should be based on qualitative identifiers, not quantitative ones. That is to say, it is more important that you feel interested or eager *enough* to begin. For example, when getting into Alignment, it's not important to feel *the most* eager you have ever felt in your life. You don't have to be jumping up and down on the bed. Feeling good enough to begin is good enough. Likewise, when you are at the Allowing step, exactly how many ideas you have isn't important. It's just important that you feel like you have some abundance of exciting ones to choose from. Quantitative metrics lead to competitiveness and perfectionism, which have no place in the fruitful, creative mind. I don't encourage them in your self-assessment.

I designed this book to be flipped through, read through, browsed, and then put down. It's a resource, but the real work starts in action. Read some, put the book down, try it. This book may be the quick read you take with you to the bathroom, or it may be the pep talk that you need in the darkest hour of the night. Whatever. I'm just glad to put it all here on the page and publish it so you can read this instead of texting me at 3:00 a.m. Stop doing that. Who does that? Stop it.

Read a little of this book instead. The solution is within you, it just takes some self-exploration to retrieve. Take a deep breath and remember that this creating stuff is supposed to be fun. Text yourself a note to buy five more copies of this book to send to friends tomorrow. Then turn out the lights and go to bed, reminding yourself that tomorrow will be easier.

THE PIE-MAKING ANALOGY

I magine you are making an apple pie from scratch. And we're talking, like, totally from scratch, like a pioneer. You will need to actually grow the apple tree for your pie. So, imagine that you really love pie in this scenario and you have incredible grit and patience. In order to make this pie, there are three big parts to the process that I want you to consider. First, you're going to have to plant the seed for the tree. Then you have to let the tree grow and bear fruit. Finally, you have to harvest the apples from the tree and make that pie. The Creative Formula can be understood in three corresponding parts: Alignment, Allowing, and Articulation.

Alignment is planting the seed for the fruit tree. Now, if you're planting a tree, you don't just plop that seed down in the middle of gravel in a desert and expect it to grow, am I right? If you expect a seed to grow, you have to give it great soil, something to plug into, something to nourish it. Just like a seed, you, as a creator, need a place you can take root and be nourished and open in order to let yourself grow upwards. You also want to give that seed ample space from other plants. Just as some plant species like to be closer together whereas some like to be more spread out, people too have different needs for the company of others or for space alone, undisturbed. Planting a seed is giving it optimum conditions to spread its roots, open up, and grow. In the same way, when you align before you create, you are surrounding yourself with great nutrition—mentally, physically, environmentally—and getting yourself in the mood to focus on the project at hand.

The second part of the Creative Formula is **Allowing**. This is the stage where you are really following your trail of interest and engaging in creative play. In this phase of the process, the goal is to keep yourself absolutely open to all ideas in order to have a lot of them. So, if Alignment is like planting a seed, then Allowing is letting the fruit tree grow. The focus is on nurturing and abundance. Typically, the first ideas you have aren't so great, so it's important to continue to have as many as possible and not to just pick the first one. It would be like picking off a piece of fruit before it's ripe, or expecting a tree to bear fruit before it has grown branches. Letting the tree grow, letting it spread its branches, is like allowing yourself to mess around in the studio, get some momentum, try out different directions, and grow lots of fruit.

Imagine trying to make a delicious pie out of tart, underripe fruit. It will alter the taste of the pie no matter what else you add to it. In the same way, it's necessary to let our ideas ripen; to let them play, stretch, and grow until they hang heavy on the tree and are clearly ready for plucking.

Articulation is what some people might call the actual art-making process. It's where meaning is made and your work becomes a clear transmission of ideas. This is the editing process. You make choices about what stays and what goes. You look at your well of work from the creative play phase and you find unifying themes or an idea that wants to come forward more clearly than the rest. You begin shedding the parts that don't match up. If Alignment is planting the seed and Allowing is letting the fruit tree grow, Articulation is choosing which fruit to pick from the tree, bringing in the harvest, and making that pie. It can be the most complex of the three parts because there is a lot involved: making choices, organizing, adding, assembling, and finally polishing that piece to perfection in the same way that you would pick the fruit, cut it up, add spices and other ingredients, stir it all together, and finally bake it.

Articulation is the set of skills that art schools are selling. They're concerned with teaching the tools in the kitchen, showing you different recipes other people have made, and basically teaching you how to bake. Some composition or choreography programs might also include some techniques for Allowing in the form of improvisational tools. But what many graduate art programs miss out on, and what most dance teachers and music teachers overlook, is teaching you about Alignment: the place where everything begins.

BEGIN WITH ALIGNMENT

Can you imagine the plight of the seed? It is small, hard, and quite tough. It's a tiny, compacted vessel that has a future tree stuffed into it. When activated, the life that spews from it is truly inspiring. Knowing nothing whatsoever about how to plant itself properly, knowing nothing about the possibilities contained inside of it, you can imagine the disposition of such a seed and its dependence on certain elements. Can you imagine this seed daydreaming of becoming a tall fruit tree, huge and stretching toward the sun, bearing sweet, delicious fruit? And even more ridiculous still, can you imagine this tiny, hard seed believing that it can become a pie?

It is preposterous, and yet this is what we expect of our artists, our tough little seeds. We expect them to grow into fruit trees and make us some pie.

"Make us some pie, Artist!"
"Turn yourself inside out, grow roots, grow branches, bear fruit, and bake your ideas to perfection!"
"We want pie!"
"More pie!"

We expect this even when we don't even teach the artist how to plant. We don't even empower creators to grow roots and be nourished by the earth, wind, sun, and rain. In the following chapters, I'll share with you step by step about Alignment, Allowing, and Articulation. I'll show you how to plant in the best places and how to allow your ideas to grow, as well as how to pick the right fruit, cut it up, and bake it to perfection. I'll give you tools and resources for baking your creative pie right away, as well as tips for keeping up with the creative process once you are finished with a project. We will also review a very practical method in applying Alignment, Allowing, and Articulation to your own work in the studio, in the classroom, in groups, and in coaching people one on one, and even in performances on stage.

But before we ever step into the creative studio, before we ever make choices about what to focus on, we must plant that seed in the right place. We must Align.

Step 1: Planting the Seed

Alignment

Definition: Warming up, practicing technique exercises, meditation, breathing, and otherwise tuning the body, mind, and heart in order to elicit a sense of eagerness for the task at hand.

Things You Can Do to Align

Warm up

Practice technique exercises

Run scales

Review a score silently

Mouth the words in your script on the way to rehearsal

Watch inspiring videos

Read books

Play acting games

Work on a character study

Practice vocal warm-ups

Meditate

Breathe

Organize your calendar

Jot down ideas

Lay out your costumes the night before a show

Eat your breakfast

Get a massage

Take a nap

Acknowledge something you like about your partner

Acknowledge yourself

Watch a video of your previous work that you like

Read through an old journal

Research an idea

Prepare

Listen to inspiring music on the way to class

Make a list of positive aspects of yourself

Make to-do lists

Put your concerns down on a list so you feel free from them

Practice self-love

Practice radical acts of self-care

Go for a hike

Ask, "Why do I love this?"

Great teachers know about alignment instinctively and convey it by example through their passion toward their topic. Sometimes we can find ourselves in alignment easily, and for us, this yields happiness and an excitement to work.

Have you ever tried to get yourself to do something when you didn't feel like it? Is there anything worse? It blows my mind how little alignment is addressed correctly in the arts. Doing creative work or practicing can feel like pushing a boulder up a hill. We simply don't feel like it because we aren't aligned, but we are probably not aware of that being the problem. The mind is playing huge games on us and telling all kinds of stories—and so we don't know what to do to get in alignment to be functional. Alignment can stem from many activities, but the goal is always the same: to cultivate eagerness.

Alignment is very simply measured by the feeling of eagerness toward the task at hand.

Isn't it nice to know that there is a piece of the creative process that comes before you even generate an idea? I find the idea of alignment comforting. If I say to you, "Create something!" you may feel a lot of pressure and not feel much like creating anything at all. You can feel overwhelmed. But if I say to you, "Scratch around, daydream, read a book, watch a video, breathe, relax, let yourself get in the mood," then you might start to enjoy yourself and come around to the idea of creation, and the flow of many ideas will begin.

You've probably already had some experience with alignment when you were growing up and learning your craft, although it's likely it wasn't a completely realized process. It's likely no one called it *alignment*, or pointed out what you were doing with an awareness of your mental state. Technique exercises, warm-ups, marking choreography, reviewing the score silently, playing acting games; these are all actions that move us toward alignment. But our education as artists often leaves out the mental shift in consciousness that is an integral part of alignment.

DESIRE IS THE SKILL YOU ARE LOOKING FOR

In all the years I've been teaching dance, of all the students I've seen, I've been most impressed by the artists who want to create more than anything else— by the brilliance of their hot desire. Perfect toes, clean turns, skillful theatricality: these are impressive to watch, and they are important. Good technique is like speaking clearly. If you have the language, you are more capable of articulating what you want to say. But when I watch dancers, I'm not just looking for technique. I'm looking for the ones who want it most. This is an indication of alignment. These are the dancers who are also artists. These artists find a way to use what skills they do have and make performances that are thrilling to watch.

These artists with hot desire are also sometimes the emotionally tortured ones. They want it so badly, and it may not have come easily at first, or they may have endured unusual hurdles and challenges. Having felt the intense rush that comes from the creative process once, they demand it of themselves always, but haven't figured out how to get in there and have it when they want.

Alignment. Desire.

We take it for granted that if a creator "really has the passion!" then they will always be driven to create. We just expect it of them and assign them mysterious and elusive muses that make creation all the more confounding and slippery to generate.

Alignment isn't as elusive as we think, but there are several ways that we hold ourselves apart from it, usually by means of the ugly monster of self-criticism.

TAMING THE MONSTERS: DEALING WITH SELF-CRITICISM

If you're feeling very judgy about yourself, then you aren't in alignment and you probably don't feel all skippity-doo-dah about going into the studio to work on something creative. Because self-criticism is such a huge hurdle that can get in the way of your creativity, and because it can block your willingness to begin a project, I'd like you to start investigating this right away in order to manage it. Self-criticism is a bad habit that is an epidemic in our society—but that doesn't mean you have to do it. When you criticize yourself or are harsh with yourself, the constant nagging can really drag you down and hold you back over time. With awareness and a few tools, it is possible to consciously shift these internal voices and learn to have a healthier dialogue with yourself. This will not only feel better to you, but will also begin to shift the way others view you as well.

SELF-CRITICISM BLOCKED ME FROM STEP 1 OF THE CREATIVE FORMULA: ALIGNMENT

At one point during my struggle with self-criticism, I had a really strong bout of performance anxiety because I had gained twenty pounds. I had had to leave my free and happy life of dancing in the studio for three to five hours every single day to go work a temp job that had lots of high-calorie snacks and free lunches lying around. At the time, it felt crushing to my soul. I felt like I had lost my home. The self-criticism that followed from that weight gain was so evil. I didn't want to make dance, I didn't want to move and feel my body, and I sure as heck didn't want anyone watching me dance. So, I was blocked from my alignment. If you are beating yourself up over your body or anything else, you're not aligned. You don't feel like making art or being creative because every step you take is full of doubt and thoughts like "Ugh, I don't know if I want to be doing this. No one wants to see me do this."

With some awareness and therapy at one point, I realized I was always saying to myself, "I'm anxious! I'm so anxious!" I was anxious about being anxious. Imagine if there were an actual physical person walking around behind me saying this all day. I had been holding myself hostage with my own thoughts the whole time. When I realized this ominous shadow of self-doubt had been following me, a lightbulb went off and I was able to redirect my thoughts.

Self-criticism can be such a paralyzing thing. It works so fervently against us, and yet we are surrounded by it on a daily basis. Just look around yourself. How many people do you see casually throwing out negative self-critical things about themselves? Probably a lot. It's a social epidemic, and it's no surprise if you suffer from this. Nearly everyone does to some degree. It takes so much courage to be an artist, especially a performing artist, because you wear your art on your person. But there are definitely ways around it. You can overcome the negative thoughts in your own head and go out there and do the work. Creating the new patterns of thought necessary to be an artist in the world isn't just about creating work; really, you are showing up and being a thought leader in the world we live in.

TIPS FOR SHIFTING YOUR BAD SELF-CRITICAL HABITS

A belief is just a thought that you keep thinking.

—Abraham-Hicks

1. Recognize when you're having a negative thought. A lot of times we just think it's normal or a part of the way we should think. We convince ourselves that we are being humble—that's a fallacy. Be light about it when you recognize a negative thought. You don't want to have a negative thought and then beat yourself up about it. That's a slippery slope to nowhere good. So recognize it, but try not to place any judgment value on it.

2. Once you recognize the negative thought, give it a name. It's helpful if it's a silly name, like "Negative Nelly." I worked with one musician in particular who found she had a continuous voice telling her that things were simple, and yet she still couldn't do those things. "It's simple! It's simple!" the voice would chide her—so we characterized that voice as "Simple Sam."

3. Don't give it actual vocal significance. Recognize this voice, call it by that silly name in your head, but don't say out loud the nasty words that it is telling you. There is so much power in the spoken word. As soon as you speak it, someone else can hear it. And what do we like to do when we hear someone bitching about something? We like to bitch too! There's nothing like a good bitch session! Suddenly the energy that could go into creating starts to take on momentum for the negative thoughts pouring out. You end up feeling crappy and unmotivated.

4. Come up with a soothing catchphrase. From a place of deep love for yourself, you're going to find a few words that you can throw in to self-soothe when you're having a negative thought. It doesn't have to be complicated. The simpler, the better. My catchphrase is often, "Ah well!" It's not patronizing; I say it in my soothing voice. This catchphrase does not make a big deal out of anything. Feel for something that sounds right to you.

5. Focus on your work. If you're thinking about your work and interested in what you're doing, there is no room for negative thoughts. The idea with these tips here is that you overcome negative thoughts just enough so that you can turn your attention to your work. Once you do that, then that focus takes on energy and power. You feel so compelled by what you're doing that there is less room for self-criticism.

My desire for you is for you to be so in love and self-obsessed and excited about what you are creating that you just don't have room for those negative thoughts. They might be there in the background or pop up from time to time, but for the most part, you are focused on your work. The more interested you are, the more ideas show up.

THE ONE AND ONLY VOICE TO HEAR

We've picked up thought patterns along the way from everyone around us and likely carry around hundreds of other people's voices in our heads. Some of these voices are those of people who have told us in some way that we aren't good enough. Other people's voices—teachers, lovers, parents—become part of our internal landscape. When we hear self-criticism, it is often just a repeating pattern of things we have heard from someone else. If you are able to move all of those other voices out of your head, you'd be left with nothing but strength and love. Your deep inner voice is supporting you. If you have a repeating thought that's mean or critical, that's not even you. It does not make sense for your inner voice to inflict harm. The criticism you hear is not from you; rather, it's just a bunch of baloney you've absorbed over the years.

That's how we know what is our true voice and what is not. And that's how we can learn to listen to the one voice, the only voice that matters.

People don't listen to a music CD because it's going to make them a lot of money. They don't go to a performance thinking it will give them a smaller waistline! Seriously. There are some key things that people are willing to pay money to consume—but art doesn't always fall into these things. It nourishes them on a deeper level—an incredibly needed level. And people do go out and find it. It's what people are seeking when they download a new song. It's what people are seeking when they read their Facebook newsfeed.

They are seeking to fill the hole in their lives that only art, music, dance, performance, and all things inspirational can fill. So what you're doing—you, Ms. Creator or Mr. Performer—is nourishing in a different way. This means that the more aligned your creation is, the more in tune and clearly articulating some deep part of *you* it is, the more it will resonate with others, and the easier it will be for them to find it.

> So wait a minute, Holly. Are you telling me that the more I
> communicate something deeply personal, something deeply
> specific from inside myself, the more I communicate with everyone?

Yes, that's the only way you communicate with *anyone*. Playing or dancing to things you have no connection to, doing what you assume you "should" do, speaks to no one. Most people are ruled by their thoughts of "I should be doing this, not that." Most people are walking around and letting that sense of obedience take over their lives. The last thing they want to see is an artist doing that too! You as an artist have this wonderful terrible wonderful freedom and duty to explore and be truthful to what you want to be doing, how you want to be doing it, and why you want to be doing it!

Alignment can sometimes be the lonely inner work of the creator. No one knows whether you've done it or not. No one else but you can truly know if you are in alignment or not. And no else but you knows what you should really be doing.

The old paradigm in arts education has always had an emphasis on looking for approval from your teacher—looking outside of yourself for that sense of self and worth. Naturally, it makes sense to have a teacher who can hand over the baton of the ins and outs and fine details of your craft. But, at a certain point, the emphasis in education should move back toward the artist's becoming more self-sufficient in their ability to create and thrive from a healthy self-awareness. Educators should teach them self-trust, an ability to observe and measure their own improvement, and the skill of finding aesthetic pleasure in their own projects.

These are skills we need to master just as much as playing the perfect note, for without them there could come a day when we don't feel like playing *any* notes, and we would have no inner tools to pull ourselves out of the fog. Too many creatives seek out approval from everywhere else and then wonder why they are confused and scattered inside about what to do next. They are letting themselves be pulled in a hundred directions, when the one piece they should be concerned with is their own alignment. As I like to say,

"I don't trust anyone who doesn't trust me to trust myself."

Ultimately, while having great collaborators and partnerships with teachers and other artists is important, you must always go back and center yourself from within. Trust your gut.

Once you free yourself from the drain of critical thought and from the invasion of so many other people's voices, you will find yourself with energy and space! All kinds of space! This is where the real fun begins, because now you can focus on the wild and sexy animal of inspiration!

INHALATION AND EXHALATION

All of us creatives have, to some degree, a pattern of taking in information by gathering resources and inspiration, and then the need to output information by creating something or performing. Much like the organic system of inhalation and exhalation, the artist inhales inspiration and exhales creativity. After I've spent months producing a project or performing for a big show, sometimes I'll find myself going inwards—wanting to take in new information and not be putting myself out there. This can be a tricky state, because it can sometimes look a lot like vegging out, and can turn into the guilty pleasure of hours of Netflix videos if I'm not careful.

INSPIRATION IS FERTILIZATION

What I've determined is that this hibernation of sorts isn't necessarily a bad thing. I just need to be more careful about what it is and which materials and resources I choose to allow in. Whatever I'm inhaling—be it books, other art, music, conversations, community, or places I go—is the soil that's going to nurture the next seed. Anything that goes into the soil gets soaked into the seed and pulled up through the roots, and plays a large role in determining the quality of the fruits of my creative work. I want to make sure I start with good things to inhale.

Of course all of us are taking in info and putting out info continuously. It's not always in large cycles over months. It can be in one sitting. It happens in verbal conversation, for example: we are listening (inhaling) and talking (exhaling). And there are bigger cycles. We are in constant conversation with the world, our environment, our communities, and other people.

I spent most of my life from the time I can remember until I was about twenty-eight years old studying how to move like someone else. It was a loooong inhale, probably not unlike many artists who study under this teacher or that master, wanting to learn all they can to be great. About ten years ago, something in me said, "Enough!" It was time to exhale, and as I listened more to this voice, ideas and movements began to pour out. It was like I'd been inhaling my whole life and was bursting to exhale. So I exhaled for a loooooooooong time. I exhaled so loudly I may have even been offensive in my belligerence. This nice Indiana girl finally got her a healthy dose of rebellion in the form of many bold creative acts!

It was a relief, but it became clear to me that I shouldn't wait so long to exhale next time, and I was going to need to inhale again at some point.

"Take a deep breath, Holly!"

There may be a more balanced approach to all this. Inspiration is a cycle of inhalation and exhalation and you must learn to take regular deep breaths. Sometimes you are drawing things close to you and your output looks weak, but just know that an exhale, a period of productivity, is right around the corner.

Alignment Exercise: Growing Roots

Besides inhaling from the outside and gathering resources from around you, there is also a way of finding inspiration from within. Asking yourself why you do what you do as a creator or a performer is a powerful method for this. If you ask these "why" questions below, you'll be able to drop right down into the heart, passion, and energy of what you do.

Connect to Your "Why"

Try filling in these blanks:

I create because . . .

I play music/dance/write in order to feel . . .

When I create/compose/choreograph, I discover . . .

What I love about my craft is . . .

What I thoroughly enjoy about it is . . .

I'm really focused on _____ because that's where _____ happens . . .

Making dance/writing songs allows me to . . .

I care deeply about . . .

TAKE ONE STEP...AND MAKE IT SMALL

Creativity is moving toward something, not away from it—and it's certainly not standing still! Sometimes you can try everything else—meditation, technique exercises, looking for inspiration—but the one thing you really need to do is just to begin.

I really believe in alignment before action. I really do. Make sure you have elicited some spark of eagerness inside before you try to do anything. It's so much easier to start if you're aligned. That being said, there will be times when you feel so twisted into a knot of stagnation that you will need to try something, anything, in order to get going.

It is better to have any motion forward than no motion at all.

This is my least favorite method of alignment. I don't like to suggest, "Just do it!" How very '90s! But I have to admit, I use it sometimes myself. I use it when I drag myself out of bed at 4:44 a.m. to write before work. I use it when I make myself do ten minutes on the treadmill at the gym. I just make myself show up. Inevitably, if I get up and look at my notes, I'll remember something I wanted to write about. Inevitably, if I spend ten minutes on the treadmill, I'll get my blood moving and feel inspired to run longer or do some weight lifting. If there's one thing you promise yourself to do, if there's one thing you want to hold yourself to as a goal, make it this:

Ask yourself to get your butt in the studio, get your instrument in your hands, or get the rough draft in front of you. Sometimes it takes showing up and going through the motions to get the engine started.

I like to think of creativity as a dynamic migration of thought, like a flock of birds. It's always moving and evolving, expanding, diversifying, diving and soaring. Creativity is never standing still. It's never waiting for us. If we want a piece of it, we've got to get our wheels spinning so we can catch up to it. We've got to give creativity the opportunity to move through us.

ALIGNMENT EXERCISE: SMALL STEPS YOU CAN TAKE

WHAT FEELS GOOD

Put on your shoes, pick up your instrument—what is the most pleasurable thing you can possibly imagine to dance, play, sing, or speak? Something in your repertoire, perhaps, or even a phrase you just learned that feels good to you. Don't worry if it's not what you feel like you "should" be working on. You are just using it to get started. Work your way through that phrase/piece/section. Now do it again and do it veeerrrrry slowly. Work through the notes, the steps, or the action at about a quarter of the speed. Or try taking the music or dance completely out of tempo and play it freely, elongating notes as you like. Savor them. Listen, feel, watch for the parts that you really love and investigate them, get inside them, see if you can really discover something new about them. Get specific about what you enjoy most.

10 Minutes a Day

For one week, try creating only ten minutes a day. It's best if this is something you can do when you first get up, before anything else. Make sure you have some kind of exercise on hand or a little creative game to try. Set a timer for ten minutes. When the timer goes off, stop what you are doing and don't pick it up again until the next day when you have your next ten minutes. I love this exercise because I feel like what makes it so tough for so many of us to start creating is that we've lost trust with ourselves that we can actually start doing the work. By showing up little by little, in small easy ways, this exercise will help you build trust with yourself quickly.

Meet the Alien

Imagine your instrument is an alien that just landed here from a far-off universe. Whether your instrument is a musical instrument, your body, your voice, a pen, or whatever, it asks you to pick it up and play with it. Pick up your instrument and run your hands over it. Explore it as though you've never seen it before. It's trying to tell you something, but you can't hear it. Put it up to your ear. Nope, still can't make out what it's saying. Then you understand what it's asking of you. You put your mouth or hands on it and begin to make a sound or move, listening very carefully all the while. Try to make out the meaning, the message beneath the sounds you normally listen to. If you are a dancer or your body is your instrument in some way, then you do this exercise the same way, listening to and feeling your arms, your legs, your spine. Become the alien life force you are exploring. Try to understand its message.

ALIGNMENT WITH A TASK: LIKE DREAMING ABOUT EATING A PIECE OF CHOCOLATE

Sometimes we can feel aligned within ourselves in a general way—generally happy, excited about life—and yet still not be in the mood to do the task at hand. We don't want to wait for the lightning of inspiration to strike us because if we're pretty happy, then there are some of us who would just never bother! It isn't enough sometimes to feel aligned *in general*, we have to get specifically aligned with a task in front of us, with the thing that we need or ultimately want to do.

I like to use the example of eating a piece of chocolate. I don't know about you, but I love my chocolate! Imagine you have a piece of chocolate you are about to eat. It's your favorite type of chocolate. Maybe that means it is raw and organic or really good for you. Whatever it is, you are super aligned with this piece of chocolate. All day you think about going home and eating it. You know it's going to be tasty in your mouth and you can just imagine the feel-good endorphins that are going to go trickling up to your brain from the chemistry of the chocolate itself. You think about the natural ingredients and all the test studies that say chocolate is so nutritious for your brain— chocolate is practically a food group! You are just completely aligned with this piece of chocolate and the eating of it.

Did you notice what's missing in the above scenario? I'm not thinking about how many calories the chocolate has, or the fact that it has sugar. Nor do I consider not eating it close to bedtime because it will cause me to wake up at 3:00 a.m. Or about the fact that there is only one piece left, and I'll likely have to sneak it past my son so he doesn't notice I'm eating it. I'm not thinking about the negative aspects of the chocolate. I'm aligning with the task of eating it by focusing only on the positive aspects.

You think about what you like about that chocolate. You think about how good it will feel to have it. You think about what it will do for you. The same goes for any task that you may have to come into alignment with when you create.

Just because we are passionate about creating or performing doesn't mean that we are eager to tackle each and every aspect of it at all times. There are times we just don't feel like practicing. There are times we'd rather climb into bed than go out and perform for people. There are times when we have to pretend that the task at hand is like eating a piece of chocolate, and get into alignment with it.

PULL UP YOUR BIG-ARTIST PANTIES

You may think you have a good handle on your self-criticism. You've been practicing and redirecting your self-critical thoughts. You feel generally positive. You're flying along in a bubble of self-love, feeling great about your work, your performances, or your next big thing. Then, one day, you find yourself in a new situation, a new class, or with new people. All that you've worked on in your head is challenged. You're performing at a festival and see an artist with a similar aesthetic to you, they blow you away with their skill, and you start to feel the old self-critical monster step out of the shadows and begin to take over. You don't want to feel this, but you do. This is when your new alignment will be tested, and you gotta pull up your big-artist panties and learn to do these two things:

1. Appreciate

and

2. Be Interested in Others

STOP COMPARING YOURSELF AND START APPRECIATING!

Typical for someone growing up in the 1980s, I was trained in the Western canon of dance: I learned ballet, tap, jazz, and modern dance, in that order of importance. By the time I was twelve, with hips and a "lady body," I knew I would never make it in the professional ballet or modern dance world. In those young years of my life, before YouTube even existed, I didn't realize there were any other options. It wasn't really until I moved to the Bay Area when I was twenty-three and saw what local artists were doing with flamenco that I even began to think of a career in dance again. Eventually, I revisited modern and contemporary dance classes to reunite with the technique, flexibility, and freedom of movement those dances allowed. By the time I did, I was inching toward thirty and a good five or ten years older than everyone else in class. No matter how creatively I was working, I was surrounded by very athletic young bodies doing very impressive things with their creativity.

I cannot lie. At times, this felt very discouraging. Although I didn't want a career as a modern dancer—so it shouldn't even have mattered!—it was difficult not to compare myself to the lithe young athletes surrounding me. So, I learned to do two things during this time: I learned to open myself up to appreciating the dancers around me without comparison to myself, and I learned to be interested in what they were doing and let that spark new ideas and open up what I thought possible for myself. Instead of thinking how different I was, I allowed myself to be curious about them. I got interested in them. I came into alignment with my experience in the class, and the doors of allowing and creativity were opened to me.

Alignment can happen in an instant, or it can take days. It depends on how long you hold out on yourself. How long are you willing to resist? How attached to your self-criticism and negative thoughts and stories are you? I could have held onto the story of being "old" for a long time and never reaped the heaps of inspiration from that experience with those younger dancers. Many artists hold on to negativity, and it wreaks havoc on their own movement forward. They have abandoned and fallen out of love with themselves in that moment, and they hold themselves away from the good stuff.

Alignment is natural. It's a healthy state of being that we would live in most of the time if we didn't concern ourselves with negative thoughts. That is to say, most people walking around are not in alignment! But this is of no concern to you, Brilliant Artist, for you have the power to reimagine the world. It just takes practice. The more you practice it, the easier it becomes. The more you focus yourself in ways that create alignment for you and stop engaging in bad mental habits, the more you will find yourself easily aligned.

YOU ARE ENOUGH

And finally, let your mental state of alignment be the win for a while. Instead of worrying about whether or not your ideas are any good, it is your mental state that should first be mastered. Take the time to find that feeling of eagerness, excitement, and creative seduction, and the juicy ideas will follow.

ALIGNMENT
SELF-ASSESSMENT QUESTIONS

- ✓ Am I eager to begin?
- ✓ Are ideas beginning to flow to me?
- ✓ Is my focus on the task at hand?

SEGUE TO STEP 2

- ✓ What am I most excited about here?

STEP 2: LETTING THE FRUIT TREE GROW

ALLOWING

Definition: Improvisation, creative play exercises, saying yes, and otherwise focusing on your trail of interest to allow an abundance of ideas to flow to you and through you.

We can all conjure up the stereotype of the creative person. They're the artsy type with notebooks filled with ideas. They have several half-finished art projects lying around their house, and when you ask them, "Whatchya working on?" their eyes light up, and you are engulfed by their energetic outpouring of ideas. You never know what kind of outfit they're going to show up wearing at any given occasion; it all depends on their artistic inclination on that particular day. They never seem to know what time it is, and when you talk about balancing their checkbook, their eyes glaze over in confusion. They can give you the best and most thoughtful birthday presents—or nothing at all. This is the allowing energy; it's what we romanticize all of our artists as having. Even if it can often be the most fun, Allowing is only one element of three that are essential to the Creative Formula.

Allowing is the ingredient defined by its spaciousness. Allowing is a nonjudgmental expansion of time. It is the freedom to grow, a space to play, and permission to hang loose, fool around, goof off, and see what comes up next. It is spontaneity. A lot of people might call it improv. It's where the origination of an idea happens. As Tina Fey says in her book *Bossypants*, "Yes, you're going to write some sketches that you love and are proud of forever—your golden nuggets. But you're also going to write some real shit nuggets. …You can't worry about it. As long as you know the difference, you can go back to panning for gold on Monday." Allowing is really mining for the gold and letting fruit grow so that when you try to actually put something together into "art" or a "product," you have good ripe ingredients with which to work.

If Alignment has the personality of a loner, self-contained and working internally, then Allowing is a social butterfly. It's playful, fun, raucous, irreverent, and carefree. In a state of allowing, you might get on the nerves of people who are not totally in a state of allowing at that moment. You may encounter others in a state of wanting to get it done (Articulation), and find them saying things like "Let's get down to business now" and "Let's get serious about this." But Allowing knows that the fruit isn't ripe yet, nor is Allowing adamant about picking the fruit off the tree prematurely. Allowing is fecund, and its fruit will fall off the tree when it's ready. There's nothing serious about ripe fruit. It's just full and ready to go when it's damn well ready.

Some of us have well-developed allowing skills. We love that feeling of being on the edge, of reaching out way up high toward the sun, falling, and seeing where we land. It's risky, wild, and sometimes messy, and we sink our teeth into it. Others might wish we could just skip this part altogether and simply think it through, organize, and come up with a finished piece. Allowing is a skill that can be developed with practice, even for the organizers and more linear-minded among us. Every single one of us, from the time we are very small, knows how to play. That is where we must start—with play. Let the games begin!

THINGS YOU CAN DO TO ALLOW

Engage in creative play exercises
Play acting games
Follow your trail of interest
Make a mind map
Listen to music and let the movement come naturally
Improvise
Try something new
Jot down ideas
Brainstorm
Go for it
Just go with it
Make your partner "right" onstage
Say yes
Pan for gold
Dig for ideas
Meander
Get lost on a long walk
Hold space

PLAY THE GAME

Creativity has to begin somewhere, and as I've discovered through years of asking people to create, it goes best if you give people some guidelines, a framework, somewhere to funnel their creativity. You don't just shout "Go!" While getting into alignment is the first step in the Creative Formula, it doesn't generate the actual fruit of inspiration. The tree still needs a little more water before it can bear fruit.

For Allowing to generate ideas, it helps if there is a problem or an assignment, a place to focus, and a thing to say yes to. The majority of books today on the topic of creativity are primarily addressing this problem, and they provide wonderful resources to any type of creative. Most of these creativity books are a compilation of different types of creative exercises you can use just to get the ball rolling. If you are just starting your creative work, or if you are between pieces and scratching around for something completely new, then I recommend having a few of these "101 Creative Exercises"–type books around. I like Tyler Christensen's *The Creativity Challenge*. I also get a lot of ideas from Anne Bogart and Tina Landau's *The Viewpoints Book*. Leaf through one of these types of books or use the exercises in this one until you find an exercise that your mind starts to reach for like a kid reaches for a particular color of crayon. Essentially, you are poking around until you find something that immediately begins sending you ideas—something you will say yes to.

CREATE YOUR OWN GAMES

As you gain experience in the area of Allowing, or have pieces you are working on, I suggest creating some of your own games. For example, if you are tasked with creating a theatre piece on the topic of *kids* and *home*, then simply using *kids* and *home* as your starting place for Allowing would be too vague and not fertilizing enough. I recommend that instead you come up with your own games based on areas of investigation you need to explore.

Simply jotting down words of association with *kids* and *home* might be one of the games. Another might be moving around the stage as if you are a kid and exploring the kid experience in a pretend kid body. In that game, you might give the kid a specific task to do in the home, or you might pretend to experience walking home as a kid. In this way, you are giving yourself a well of discovery to water your starting place, while also creating a plethora of movement vocabulary to build to your specific work. You are also likely to encounter more questions and more associations that keep your work flowing.

My Favorite Five Allowing Exercises

There are infinite amounts of effective creative exercises out there, and I implore you to discover them through books, other creatives, or the Internet. I'm always making up and discovering new ones, but here are my favorite five that just about any type of creator or performer can use:

1. Create Something Terrible

It's exactly like it sounds. I want you to make a bad dance, a bad song, a bad monologue, a bad anything, depending on what you do. Don't overthink it. What does *bad* mean to you? Put together pieces of the worst things you've ever seen or heard, or dive deep within to bring life to your crappiest ideas. Create something terrible! And make sure it's awful, whatever that means to you! The beautiful thing about this game is that it addresses your fears directly by forcing yourself to attempt to do the very thing you are afraid of.

2. Breakin' the Rules

Part 1: Take out a fresh sheet of paper. At the top right of the page, write "Rules of [Whatever You Do]." It might be "Rules of Belly Dance Choreographies," "Rules of Classical Music," "Rules of Musical Theatre," or even "Rules of My Own Personal Style of Songwriting."

Whatever you are doing, whether or not you are aware of it, there are rules and assumptions we live within and even embed within us. Sometimes we don't even realize how much these confine us. On the left side of the paper, just start listing all the rules you can think of.

Here's an example:

Rules of Classical Ballet

- starts on 1
- always dance to the music
- must have pointed feet

- phrases must resolve with the music
- shoulders back
- head up
- posture straight
- must keep face serene
- the dance helps move the story along
- must have a beginning, middle, and end
- shouldn't stop moving and take breath in middle of phrase
- should look pretty
- no shouting
- no fidgeting
- piece should build to climactic point

Try to at least fill the page all the way down to the bottom on the left side with rules. At first, you will list obvious rules, but as you keep going it will get harder. Maybe you'll dig up some assumptions you never even faced before. Try to dig for those. A seed needs good depth in the ground to take root!

Part 2: Make a sketch breaking at least one of the rules. When I use the word *sketch*, I'm using it to mean something made quickly, without too much deliberation. Don't worry about making a finished product, just get something down, whether it's a sketch of a dance, a sketch of a tune, or a sketch of a scene. Use this rule-breaking as an exploration. Try to do more than just dip your toes into breaking the rule. Try to commit to breaking that rule and fully exploring what might be really interesting there in your sketch.

3. Five Puzzle Pieces

Part 1: For this game, you only get to use five notes (or five movements, five words, five gestures, or five sounds). The process of choosing which five pieces shouldn't be too overthought. You are not trying to sort out how you will use them, and in fact, if you already have an idea of what they will become, then go back and choose different pieces. The objective is that you have no idea how these five puzzle pieces will come together. Just reach for things you feel drawn to work with—pieces that seem fun to you right now.

Now get crystal clear on those five pieces. Repeat them to know them. Jot them down on a piece of paper to remember what they are. Draw a quick picture, remember how they feel in your body, give them names like Roger, ChiChi, and Russell. Maybe they remind you of a smell. Stretch yourself to remember them with all five senses: smell, taste, touch, sight, and sound. Maybe one note is quick, maybe the other is fervent. The more distinct and crystal clear they are, the better. The more ways in which you can latch onto them to remember them, the better.

For example, if I were a painter, I might choose five different colors as my puzzle pieces. Or maybe I like multimedia art, so I have two colors and some aluminum foil, and I choose diagonal lines and upward strokes as my additional puzzle pieces. Once I pick these five as my puzzle pieces, I spend some time getting to know them, noticing the properties and associations of each one. The violet paint I'm using reminds me of a jacket I never wear, so I refer to it in shorthand as "Daring Lady." The black color I've chosen feels very final, and I take note of its somewhat piercing quality, and how it feels foreboding to me. The aluminum foil carries a faint tinny smell with it, and by handling it, I'm adding crinkling sounds to this experience. When I think of making upward strokes I feel hopeful, but I notice that the repetition of movement makes my wrist get sore. Diagonal lines make me think of bridges and triangles and things that are strong, which reminds me of my ex, and so I dub those lines "Marcus."

<u>Part 2</u>: Make a sketch using only these five pieces. Play around with them and move them around in multiple ways. These are things that you were drawn to for a reason. Don't just string them together aimlessly. Commit to exploring combinations of these five pieces and be open to learning something from the experience of seeing them together in different ways.

4. A FIVE-PART STUDY OF ONE GEM

This exercise draws on Daria Halprin's communication feedback model.

<u>Part 1</u>: Cultivating the Gem—One Movement, One Gesture, One Short Phrase, One Musical Hook, or One Line

Imagine that your body is very, very wise, and it's a treasure trove of secrets, gold, and gems that have been locked away, but long to be found. Imagine yourself like an explorer in the treasure cove that is your body. Start with your breath. Close your eyes and breathe, and imagine that if you clear your mind, a gem will float from the depths of your body and speak to you some beautiful phrase it's been longing to say. Take a deep breath; take a moment to really feel into your body, your feet, your legs, pelvis, belly, ribcage, shoulders, neck, arms, hands, face, head. Breathe and ask your body what it would like to say, then really listen with an open mind and let yourself be surprised by the answer.

Allow a short phrase or short series of movements to arise, no longer than five seconds long.

The important piece of this exercise is to keep your movements, or musical phrase, just the right length—no longer than three to five seconds long. You won't be able to do much with one note, but you also won't be able to do this exercise effectively with anything that takes longer than about five seconds.

<u>Part 2</u>: Using Your Gem

Ask yourself these questions:

What is this thing?

Repeat it to know it. Repeat your movement or phrase over and over again until you really know it. Study it, noticing the nuances, where it originates, how it makes you feel, what it makes you imagine, and where you feel it in your body.

What else?

Add something to it: a gesture, a punctuation, another small movement or note; another piece to the beginning, middle, or end of it...add something.

What more? What less?

Intensify the movement or phrase. You can do this in any direction: make it louder, softer, bigger, or smaller. You are taking the movement or phrase and its inherent qualities and pushing them further and further, like a sweater being pulled out of shape. See what happens to it when you intensify it in a myriad of ways.

How else? Can it go another direction?

Redirect the movement or phrase. Change direction, flip it inside out, redirect it from one body part to another, from instrument to voice. Is it all in one place? Take it across the room. Redirect.

Why not?

Integrate all the different variations that you explored with the questions above. As you do this, you'll find your judgment mind begin to take over. It will try to put things in an order that "makes sense." See if you can refrain from this by mishmashing the variations together without judgment. Ask yourself, "Why not?" Repeat the original movement or phrase, leaving the addition out, and then put it back in. Intensify and redirect. Intensify in a different way and repeat it. Without trying to make sense of it or make it into a composition per se, create a dance, song, or piece of poetry out of all the different variations—create one fluid piece that plays with them all.

5. STORY OFF THE PAGE

Flip through a book of short stories or poems, a journal, or a newspaper, and choose one story to tell. Go with the story that starts giving you ideas first. You will tell this story through song, movement, dance, tune, lyrics, spoken poetry, gesture, music, however you wish—but not written. It must be expressed through performance somehow—off the page. You don't have to create the story literally, but you can if you want. Your sketch can be a telling of the story, or a response to the story itself. It doesn't have to be a literal reenactment, but it could have elements that are recognizable. It is up to you how to approach the story.

HOW TO KEEP ALLOWING ONCE YOU'VE STARTED

When you are in a state of allowing, then you are saying yes to things, and once you've said yes, you begin a motion forward which creates momentum. Now you can pick up speed and go on forever. But don't worry. You likely won't go on forever in Allowing mode because most of us break the momentum and stop allowing in one of three major ways: we introduce fear, judgment, or anxiety into our thoughts. We let our thoughts take us out of alignment (step 1 of the Creative Formula) and we don't have access to great ideas.

> These three types of thoughts,
> fear, judgment, and anxiety,
> don't allow the movement forward because
> they are inherently resistant by nature.

If these thoughts could talk, they would have a big, fat "NO" coming out of their faces at all times. When we let these types of thoughts enter, we stop allowing and gag our inner muse until it shuts up, and we become stuck. At this point, the fruit-bearing tree that we are is in the middle of a drought.

How do we allow our muse to join the conversation again? How do we overcome the fear, judgment, and anxiety that arise when facing the creative process? Following are three keys I've discovered to lining up your frame of mind and getting your muse to confidently join you at the table more often and more consistently.

THE THREE KEYS TO ALLOWING: DISCERNMENT, PRODUCTIVE PROCRASTINATION, AND FOCUS

JUDGMENT VERSUS DISCERNMENT

Your muse loves everybody and everything, but also knows what it is that you *really* want. So if you want to be in connection with your muse, you must practice discernment instead of judgment.

The distinction between judgment and discernment is a subtle but important one. It's the difference between dismissing something by placing value on it (judgment), and simply deciding it isn't a right fit at this time (discernment). Judgment throws an anchor down into the water. Once you say something is good or bad, then you stop the Allowing process, where anything flows. Your mind starts to wonder what else is good and what else is bad. It shifts the mental landscape, casting a filter that doesn't serve the Allowing phase of the creative process. Nevertheless, there are still some light choices to be made, some decisions about which road to take, and that's where discernment comes in. Discernment is making choices without the heaviness of judgment value. Here are some examples:

JUDGMENT	DISCERNMENT
"Oh, that idea is dumb."	"That idea isn't a good fit, but it makes me think of..."
"My dance partner isn't doing it right!"	"What my partner is doing is different than I expected."
"This first draft is crap."	"This first draft is just a draft and isn't finished yet. What would benefit me most to try next?"
"That director is horrible."	"That director has a way of working that I would prefer more if we had space to explore this incredible script."
"This painting is a mess."	"This painting doesn't seem like it wants to come forward at this time as much as this other one."
"These title suggestions are all ridiculous."	"These titles aren't lighting up for me, but I like some of the words, like 'wisdom.'"

KNOWING THE DIFFERENCE

Being discerning is honoring your preferences while keeping yourself open to what might follow. It ensures a sense of flow rather than blockage. It takes blame, judgment, and personal criticism out of the picture and just acts as a filter, allowing ideas, people, experiences, and events to be sifted through as needed. It cultivates acceptance of what is, while choosing the path of where you want to go. Discerning is saying "Yes, and...."

I really like Tina Fey's idea that the creative writing process is like panning for gold. Yes, in the moment you are searching for gold, you set aside all that is not gold for that particular project. Things you might have missed, that you might have labeled, or that you might have dismissed with judgment the first time around have a value that has yet to be recognized. If you don't just chuck it off into the trash and instead value all components of the Allowing process, you might decide later to go rummaging through that pile and find some beautiful green aventurine, sturdy granite, elegant sapphires, or something else equally valuable to use for the next project.

PRODUCTIVE PROCRASTINATION

Your muse knows when things are supposed to happen. When people want to talk about the capricious nature of artistic inspiration, I give them this: ideas won't necessarily show up at the moment that you demand them, or in the manner or fashion that you would like. But, in truth, this is a good thing. If you relax just a little bit, you will find that they show up in a way that is extraordinary in its perfection. They show up in a way that you could have never consciously orchestrated had you tried. Yes, art is part craft, and practicing and preparing your skills with dedication is definitely important. Getting into alignment and showing up is important. I like to say that dance is primarily getting your butt in the studio. But practice of skills is only one element to creation. You must also practice training your mind: practice discernment instead of judgment and practice focusing on those ideas that *are* working for you. The rest of the creative process is allowing yourself to be surprised by the unfolding of the work, as opposed to attempting to manhandle it into place.

Whenever I work on a new piece, there is often the initial spark—or thread, as I sometimes call it—that gets me going, but then there is this incubation period where it feels like nothing much is happening. I'll be working on the piece in the studio, sometimes for weeks, just playing with different movement and creating a cache of movement vocabulary, taking my time in the Allowing phase. To an outsider it might not look like I am doing much, but this is the part where I'm sifting and discerning ideas, following the trail of what interests me, and researching the questions I have. At some point, things begin to fall together and there'll be one day when I feel the entire map of the thing come together and it begins to articulate. There is a bit of a rush when this happens, because in this one glorious moment I get a glimpse of the beauty and genius of the workings of it all as it snaps into place.

But I can tell you there are days when I don't go into the studio. I can feel that it will spit me out, so I go running, I write, or I meet with a friend who inspires me instead. Or I'll go to the studio, but I'll do nothing but technique exercises. Maybe I'll spend some time smoothing out a new turn that I've recently discovered. But I'm not trying to *create* anything. And I think it is important to allow yourself to do that sometimes. So, how do you know the difference between productive procrastination and just plain laziness? I think with practice and over time, you can feel the difference. You can feel when you are in a space to try to work on something, and you can feel when you are too far away and will just churn in your own frustration. If you make movement forward, any movement forward, toward your primary goal, then you will establish a trust with yourself that you are being productive. Sometimes it's more conducive to feel for the momentum and tap in when the ideas are ripe.

FOCUS ON YOUR TRAIL OF INTEREST

If you think back to a time when you felt the inspired creative rush, you may remember that it was marked by those moments when you were fully committed to what it is that interests you. The longer you are able to stay focused in this way, the longer you are working from this inspired place. It is only when you let someone or something divert your thought toward worry, fear, or anxiety that you slow yourself down in the Allowing phase. As long as you are devoted to what interests you, take it seriously, and follow the path of what is interesting or fun about it, you will be allowing. Ideas will continue to flow.

> You cannot allow when you are fearful, anxious, or judgmental.
> You can be focused or fearful.
> Not Both.

> People love to say that being an artist is overcoming your fear. But what about leaving the *overcoming* activity out of it? What if it is just about focusing somewhere else?

You only have to be courageous if you are thinking about fear. If you aren't thinking about the thing you are fearful of, then you are focused somewhere else.

The *Oxford Dictionary Online* defines *muse* as "a woman, or a force personified as a woman, who is the source of inspiration for a creative artist," but this puts the power outside of us. And while I agree that artistic inspiration may be tapping into something greater than us, I mostly think it is like tapping into the greater part of us—like plugging a lamp into an electrical outlet. There is an infinite well of power running to that lamp through that outlet, but unless the lamp is turned on, it's useless. The power is never going to flow through it and create light.

I prefer the definition of *muse* as a verb. *Merriam-Webster* provides us with this: "To become absorbed in thought; especially: to turn something over in the mind meditatively and often inconclusively." *Muse*, to me, is interchangeable with *creative genius*. It is that bigger part of yourself that is there for you always when you are focused, absorbed in thought, and meditative, accepting of an open-ended outcome.

When you are discerning, you are Allowing.

When you are letting events unfold and feeling for the best moments to work, you are Allowing.

When you feel interested, you are Allowing, and your muse is right there with you, pointing you toward the branch with all the best fruit. The buds are blossoming and their fragrance calls to you.

When you lean fully into what you love and enjoy the unfolding of the creative journey, you are inviting the full resources available to you—call it your muse, your genius, or simply all the best of you—to play in the creative process with you. The more you invite that muse and practice allowing by using discernment, productive procrastination, and focusing on your trail of interest, the more familiar and easy it will be. You will find yourself there more often enjoying the full potential of your artistic gifts.

THE IMPORTANCE OF THE WITNESS

Oh my god, that was amazing! Oh, crap...wait! What did I just do?

The wonderful thing about the Allowing phase is that all kinds of amazing ideas show up and you may find yourself playing a melody you've never heard before, generating movement that feels completely new to you, saying new lines that crackle with truth. You are truly in the zone and tapping the infinite well of creative ideas! But what can be really frustrating about this phase is trying to capture some of those new ideas so you can actually work them into the Articulation phase. I hear it from creators all the time:

Oh my god! I did this amazing thing, and I can't for the life of me remember what the frick it was!

In order to explain this phenomenon, I'd like to share a bit about what I know about consciousness and how it works with the creative mind. In my lifelong explorations of creativity and transcendent performance experiences, I've discovered two consciousness gateways that can keep us from total transcendent, mystical experiences. They help us hold our shit together so we don't just get completely blissed out and full of feels and have no real idea of what's going on. These two consciousness gateways that help us hold it together in real life are what I like to call the Editor and the Witness.

The Editor and the Witness are necessary for everyday living and for actually getting our creative work finished. They keep us grounded and moving through life. They help us get into trouble, get out of trouble, stay out of trouble, learn from our problems, and basically progress forward in life. But we do have the capacity to override them, to transcend them, and slip into the nothingness that exists beyond them. Some people call this enlightenment, becoming one with everything, or shamanic journeying. I call this mode of consciousness the Vessel.

Essentially, as you stop choosing (transcending the Editor) and you stop watching (transcending the Witness), you surrender fully and become the Vessel—mobilized by a larger, universal energy that moves through you.

Ready for the punch line? You can't finish creative work as the Vessel.

It feels good there, but it ain't gettin' done, honey!

So what's happening when you can't remember the cool thing you just did? You've slipped past your two consciousness gateways, the Editor and the Witness. In order to grab on to some of those cool ideas, you have to bring one of them back!

The last phase of the Creative Formula, Articulation, calls on the Editor heavily. In order to create, you must make choices and edit. But you don't need the Editor in order to align or allow. In fact, the Editor is an unwelcome party guest when you are trying to plant your seeds and grow juicy fruit. It's like introducing a lawn mower to plow over your baby trees. You can't start pruning your ideas before they've even given you fruit!

Sometimes, when we successfully get rid of the Editor and fall into all that spaciousness, it can get so seductive and juicy that we also lose the Witness.

The Witness is the one taking note of that really cool new thing you just did.

The moral of the story here, in the midst of all this transcendental talk, is that in order to be able to not drop your apples when you're harvesting them, you'll need to hang on to the part of you that's watching the action. You have to stay present to what's ripening and watch that fruit before it falls off the tree. You have to catch it in action before it rots.

ALLOWING
SELF-ASSESSMENT QUESTIONS

- ✓ What am I saying yes to here?
- ✓ Does it lend itself to more ideas?
- ✓ Do I still feel a forward momentum?
- ✓ Do I feel abundant, like I have a lot of choices?
- ✓ Does it still feel like an interesting mystery, yet to be solved?
- ✓ Am I still excited?

SEGUE TO STEP 3

- ✓ What am I most excited to explore?

Step 3: Making the Pie

Composition provides a structure for
working from our impulses and intuition.

—Anne Bogart & Tina Landau, The Viewpoints Book

ARTICULATION

Definition: Composing, choreographing, editing, and otherwise creating into a clear, meaningful, and unified transmission of ideas.

THINGS YOU CAN DO TO ARTICULATE

Edit

Compose

Organize

Outline

Arrange

Choreograph

Draft

Distill

Polish

Choose

Take one road over another

Design

Redesign

Perfect

Evaluate

Curate

Compile

Integrate

Articulation begins the moment you start to commit to one idea. At this point you have to trust that your interest in it is enough. Once you have aligned and allowed ideas to flow in, now you make choices about what stays and what goes. This is also known as the editing process. It's where you make meaning. It is art making. This is the full rendering of an idea.

We are, whether consciously identifying as an artist or not, choosing and composing our lives every day. One of the most glorious things about being a creative human is our ability to make choices. Freedom is so important to us that we fight for it. We are even willing to go to war for freedom so that other people can have it too. The idea of not having the freedom to choose elicits the feral animal from deep within us.

Articulation is the act of choosing that fruit, bringing it into your kitchen, cutting out the bad bits, assembling it in a way that's tasty, then baking it to perfection. It's true alchemy. Remember that tiny seed from chapter 1? Who could imagine, on first glance, that you could turn a seed into a pie? It's an involved process that requires many tools and measures, choices, and flexibility.

In this chapter, not only will we go through that process step by step, but I'll give you tools to help you make Articulation less painful and more fun—tools to open you up and let the goods become real. We'll look at not only what you do in Articulation, but how you might be able to do it better.

If you can imagine that the Creative Formula is like a pregnancy, then Alignment and Allowing are those first quiet and anticipatory months. An idea is swelling and growing bigger and bigger, until Articulation births the manifestation of your labor. It's all sweat and excitement, pain and happiness, things bursting forth, coming into full view. You are opening a part of yourself that at first seems too small to let something so big come through. The amazement that you created this big thing never leaves you, though the pain of the process quickly does. Through the blood, the breathing, and the stretching, it all becomes real.

How to Grab On to Good Ideas: Harvesting the Fruit

How often have you had a great idea for a new script, portrait, dance, sculpture, or poem one day, only to try to return to it the next and find your miraculous creation has somehow slipped away? Often our initial inspirations can be the path to something brilliant, but as I discussed in the last chapter, if we aren't using the Witness to observe landmarks to return to these ideas, then the initial desire to fully realize them can disappear. Just as important as generating great ideas is learning how to grab hold of them. Here are some ways that you can grab an idea by the thread once it surfaces:

Repeat it to know it.

The most basic of instructions, and yet the most important: Before you can even congratulate yourself, do it again. And again. And again. Sometimes a common monster that creeps into our thoughts while improvising is, "Oh, I always do that. Why do I keep repeating that? No, no. I want to do something new." But in the quest for something new, we can miss the brilliant thing we just did. Don't be afraid of repetition. It's important to help you capture things clearly.

Work on the parts that you're interested in first.

I see this all the time with the artists I coach. They have a great idea for something, but then put up roadblocks for themselves by insisting they work on the beginning, even if it was one particular scene that was thrilling to them. I always suggest working on the parts that seem to want to come forward first. Even if it doesn't seem to make sense to you, if you trust your natural trail of interest, you will allow the work to unfold in an even better way than you could have orchestrated.

Record your initial ideas on how it might develop, even if they seem too obvious.

Often our first intuition on a subject can be very insightful. It is always important to explore beyond these first ideas, of course. But sometimes those first intuitions will serve you down the road. Even if they seem obvious or pedantic, write them down. If nothing else, getting them out of your head and onto paper clears the way for more ideas to flow.

PICK A THEME SONG.

Was there a piece of music you were listening to when the inspiration came to you? Is there a song that encapsulates the feeling of what you are working on? Using a piece of music to get you back to the initial inspiration is extremely effective. For dancers or choreographers already using music, I would suggest creating an entire playlist that includes other music that may capture some aspect or idea you are developing inside the dance. Working with music other than the final music will also give your choreography or composition greater depth and texture in the end.

BUILD BRIDGES FOR THE NEXT TIME YOU WORK ON IT.

Don't stop creating when you're stuck on a section. It leaves you in the mind-set of being stuck when you think later on about a project. It is better to stop working when you have a good idea or a brief sketch of what is coming next. Stop there. Stop while you're ahead. As Twyla Tharp puts it so brilliantly in her book *The Creative Habit*, "Try to stop while you have a few drops left in the tank, and use that fuel to build a bridge to the next day." The sense of accomplishment and having an entry back into the work is key.

KEEP NOTES ON IT.

For dancers or painters or anyone else not writing, it is helpful to put down your ideas in a different modality. Jot down notes about the movements, the feeling, the idea, the desired outcome—whatever it is that caught your attention and made you want to embark on this particular project. Even if you don't look at the notes again, there is some sense of security in getting it down. It becomes more tangible, more real. As performing artists, we work in the ephemeral a lot of the time, so it's great to have the opportunity to create artifacts and interact physically with our work whenever possible.

TITLE YOUR WORK.

Give your work a few key words that describe the piece, even if it doesn't end up being the actual title of the piece. This can be crucial to remembering the feeling of it. A title also triggers your mind to take the work seriously. What was previously just a funny scene is now a full-fledged piece. When you take on your work with integrity, then ideas will show up more readily.

As you continue to come back to your project, you will want it to develop, change, and grow. You want your initial idea to expand to include more things, more dimension, more depth. But by giving yourself a road map or a thread to pull on, you'll be able to hang on to the magic of the initial inspiration that got you working on it in the first place.

Lastly, it is important to remember that nothing is ever really lost. If there is an idea that you feel slip from you, it is often something that will reveal itself again much later on, often in a more developed and precise form. Part of staying sane as a creator comes from allowing things to unfold on their own time, when they are ready, and trusting it will always work in your favor to be at peace with the process.

ARTICULATION EXERCISE: EMBODIMENT PRACTICE

When you receive that first excitement about an idea, ground it in your body right away. Take a moment to close your eyes, breathe, and ask yourself where this idea might live inside of you. What specific body part wants to move when you think about this idea? Maybe it gets your toes tapping or your head swaying. See if you can use all five senses to describe it. How does it look? Taste? Sound? Smell? Feel? What emotions does it invoke? Whatever it is, write it down as part of your road map back to working on the idea. Dancers: Be as specific as possible. Exactly how is your head swaying side to side? Are you using your whole upper torso, or just your neck? Is your body like a sapling in the soft breeze or a flag flapping in a quick wind? Your work is of the body, so nuance is most important to recapture the initial feeling of the movement.

DIVIDE AND CONQUER

Benjamin Franklin used to keep his different inventions and projects on a Lazy Susan (which he invented, by the way). A Lazy Susan is a circular turntable that folks would place in the middle of the dining table to hold and easily distribute their condiments. Instead of having to ask Cousin Lou to pass the salt, you could simply spin the Lazy Susan around to where the salt was and grab it yourself.

Benjamin Franklin used a Lazy Susan for keeping his projects organized and handy. When he would get tired, bored, or frustrated with one project, he would simply put it back on the Lazy Susan and turn it around. He would grab another project to work on until he got tired or frustrated with that, and so on and so forth. Benjamin Franklin was a hugely prolific creative. To this day we benefit from his creative genius and work as an inventor. Not to say that Benjamin Franklin didn't also perhaps have moments of overwhelm or panic, but he found a way to work with his onslaught of ideas. He set himself up for success—hell, he invented a physical object to aid in his process!

He learned to divide and conquer.

Often artists will have a tendency to feel like their brilliance must come from hard work. They slave away single-mindedly for hours on one project so as to really put in the time, and they resist their natural tendency to let their mind wander. The reality is that sometimes the wandering mind is our self-preservation kicking in or, even better, our intuitive mind suggesting a new way around a problem—a way that can be discovered by working on something else for a while. Great ideas and moments often come from taking a break.

Focus on one thing at a time.

When you first begin articulating an idea, it's important to let yourself develop pieces separately. Divide whatever you're doing into sections. Maybe they already exist in obvious phrases: you have one gesture you like, there's this really lovely across-the-floor phrase, and then you have this very clear idea for a moment between two actors onstage. Don't try to force yourself to work on putting all the parts together before you've developed each one. Sometimes this may even mean that it feels like you are working on three or four totally different pieces at once. This could be the case. Let yourself explore them separately. If you get stuck, then put that piece back on your virtual Lazy Susan, spin it, and take a stab at something different. Even if one piece ends up not working out and getting dropped from the whole, if nothing else, these separate explorations will have served to inform each other and are an important part of the Articulation process.

Ingredients: Choosing Your Variables

'Art' is not merely about representing the outward appearance of
a given subject; it is just as much about selecting its essence,
accentuating and holding it for the viewer's contemplation.
Art frames our view of a scene and freezes the moment in an ordered
beauty of line and shape, form and space, and color and tone.

—Simon Jennings, The Complete Artist's Manual

As you continue to explore the nuggets of gold you pulled out of Allowing—those pieces that sit on your Lazy Susan—you will need to get clear about what variables you want to focus on. What matters to you? What are the questions you want to explore? Creating a piece of performance art is a fantastic opportunity to create a piece from scratch in whatever way you wish to see it. Being clear about the variables that you like to play with and that you are choosing to explore in this particular piece is essential to giving your

Articulation a thread, and will make unification and clarification that much easier.

Potential Variables

Tempo

Relationships between people onstage

Speed

Breath

Lines

Curves

Dynamics

Texture

Theme

Sound

Color

Tone

Stillness

Spontaneity

Perspective

Images

Space and negative space

Gesture

Chord progression

Rhythm

Repetition (or lack thereof)

Props or objects

Instrumentation

Volume

Pitch

Duration

Momentum

Movement qualities: bold, fierce, delicate

Cross-disciplines and how they interact: how sound interacts with movement, how dance can be arranged on musicians, theatre with dance, etc.

Musical key

VARIABLES AND THE QUESTIONS YOU HAVE ABOUT THEM

It's not enough to say you are interested in rhythm. Ask yourself *how* you are interested. Are you interested in how it can punctuate an emotional moment? Are you exploring how the repetition of a rhythm can evoke a certain feeling? Or maybe you're a composer who is in love with tone. What about it is thrilling to you? What about it would you like to explore more? Maybe you know what perfect tone sounds like, but are interested in exploring how you can use imperfect tone to create an uncomfortable dissonance. You're an actor exploring gesture, and when you ask yourself *how*, you realize you're interested in the small, quiet, unconscious gestures a person makes when they're deep in thought or nostalgia. And so you begin looking for them everywhere you go, then bringing them back to the studio when you work and incorporating them into your character.

For example, when I was working on a solo I had in Ravel's *Bolero*, I wanted to do something fun and different. Although I was dancing with a flamenco company—and so flamenco was the primary movement vocabulary we were using—I had been studying modern dance again more regularly and was itching to use some modern turns and movements that would have been difficult in flamenco shoes. I also knew I was expected to dance to the music to some degree, but I wanted to challenge that just a little. The music of Ravel's *Bolero* seems very pompous. It builds with self-importance. Yet as I listened to it more and more, it seemed to not take itself too seriously. By repeating the bold theme again and again, it became almost a farce of itself in my mind. There was some cheekiness in it. And so, my variables became my bare feet, musicality, textures of sharp and soft, and comedy.

As I worked, I asked questions like:

What are the most important accents to hit and keep sharp?

How can I hit some of the accents in a surprising way, while still expressing them in a manner that satisfies the need for punctuation?

71

How can I overlap movements and move more fluidly between the accents, instead of dancing to every single note with precision?

Now that I am carefree with my bare feet, what else can I throw in there?

Now that I have a better shot at staying grounded, where can I take bigger risks and take faster turns or pitch myself off balance on purpose?

The bare feet lent themselves to comedy as well. It was just a little on the side of ridiculous to see an elegant lady all dressed up, hair and makeup sleek, then look down at the bottom of the picture and see some bare white feet. Already I'd catch the audience off guard in this otherwise very decorous production. How could I emphasize the cheekiness that I felt when I listened to *Bolero*? How could I create movements that maybe poked a little fun at flamenco or caricatured the way flamenco is viewed by those audiences outside of it?

These variables and the questions like this that they evoke create the language you'll work from throughout the creative process. They'll eventually narrow to a dialect. Having this well of vocabulary you've created makes it all the easier when you are in the final stages of Articulation and you get stuck. You can always look back through your vocabulary and pluck out just the right thing to make the final piece work, because you did the legwork of creating that in the first place.

As you diligently work on your different sections, focusing on your important variables and the questions they drive you to answer, you will begin to create a body of work. Your movement vocabulary as a choreographer, your melody as a composer, your inner world as an actor playing a character: these core pieces all begin to come into focus. You'll look up and realize there is a body of work in front of you that could really be something.

THE MIXING BOWL: PUTTING IT ALL TOGETHER

HAVE FAITH IN DISPARATE PARTS

There will come a time, every time you create something, when you feel like you are sitting in a very full room with many pieces surrounding you—almost like a messy room before a garage sale: crap everywhere, but some hidden treasures too. You are surrounded by juicy tidbits—your anecdotes, your wisdom, your poetic wordings, this gesture, that phrase—and you have absolutely no idea how it's all going to fit together cohesively. You just have a feeling it's going to be a ton of work. It can be overwhelming. This is the point where you must have faith in the disparate parts. You must believe that all those bits will fit together, and you must persist, because I can tell you that the part where it all snaps together and flows is just around the corner.

This can easily happen with larger productions, but it can even happen with smaller ones as well. I remember one instance of this when I was creating the piece *Twinkle*, which I choreographed on a group of young dancers that I had loosely dubbed the Elixir of Youth. For a period of about two years, I was blessed with the opportunity to work with the most exceptional young people, ranging in ages from twelve to seventeen. They were exceptional not necessarily because they were all the finest trained dancers, but rather because of the other skills they brought with them. Three of the boys were incredible capoeiristas and could do anything with athletic grace and fluidity. The girls had an awareness of movement rarely seen in dancers under thirty. I could have them do anything, even just raise an arm, and it was fascinating to watch. And then to top it all off, all of these dancers were ready and willing to try whatever creative thing I asked of them. Thus, this group of vivacious and gifted kids was truly an elixir of youth, inspiring youthfulness in anyone who was lucky enough to watch them dance.

When I was working on *Twinkle* with them, I was really tapping into this special sentient quality. I found that asking them to repeat a small section, as opposed to learning lengthy new choreography, led to a greater ability to really sink into the work. With a small section, they could really know it and relax into it, so rehearsals looked like a lot of repetition. I'd come to rehearsal with heaps of material, but then we'd end up working on one short phrase. I found myself caught up in their expression of the movements and would have them repeat the phrase in several different ways, changing the music, trying different groups, different orders of movements. I'd focus in on a dancer's presence, and instead of plowing through material and advancing the actual piece, I was obsessed with coaching their delivery and perfecting something small one moment at a time.

We were two weeks out from production and the dancers were starting to get a little nervous. We had a handful of beautiful phrases—and no dance. Though they trusted me, I started to sense that they were concerned about where this was headed. To tell you the truth, so was I. And then I was in rehearsal watching them rehearse the phrases we did have, one after another, and it all began to snap together. I started to understand how the phrases all fit—how the seemingly disparate parts of each phrase were actually expressing a different piece of a whole. The montages began to make sense, and I knew all of a sudden exactly how they were all supposed to go together. From there, I quickly added a couple of transitions, but otherwise *Twinkle* became a series of montages of these separate phrases. By changing the groupings and order, I created a deeper order. The organization of the phrases made the meaning. If I hadn't had faith in those disparate parts, then I may never have realized this version of the piece. I could have sloppily or haphazardly thrown them together one after another in an effort to get it done. But I had held out for the bigger vision to come to me, and it had paid off.

ORGANIZATION

It's important to have an idea of the different ways you can organize something and to know how you tend to do it. It makes it easier the next time you go to create something. If you have no idea how you organize when you are creative, then simply look to other areas of your life. How do you organize your house? Your closet? Your day? You might have the urge to jump to the conclusion of, "Oh, I'm just not very organized! I'm a mess!" But you're doing a disservice to yourself with that judgment. It's easy to revert to these self-critical and negative thoughts, like "I'm terrible at pulling things together!" Maybe you *could* be a little better at getting organized in your life. Who couldn't use some more organization? I know very few people who are perfectly organized in every area of their lives. Instead, ask yourself, "How *do* I know where to find the clean clothes? Oh yes, I put my slightly dirty clothes over the end of the bed, and the sweaty ones in the hamper. The clean stuff is on top of the dryer and the things I never wear are in the drawers."

You see, you *do* have a system of organization—whether it's helpful to your life or not. All of us, even the most seemingly disorganized among us, find a way to organize. Even if it is simply tossing the apples into the bowl every which way, that is your form of organization. "I toss every which way." Be aware of this.

The way you organize a piece will have a big effect on the way it is received. It is often a sign not only of your individual voice, but of the time period you live in or a time in history you wish to emulate or evoke. Choosing to put one simple clarifying gesture or moment between characters at the beginning of your piece will inform your audience of something. If you decided to put it at the end, the effect would be very different.

Organization should enhance your material. By being deliberate about your organizational choice, you can give your piece the feeling of continuity, order, and inevitability; build to a conclusion; create dramatic variety; embellish one idea, revealing more and more depth with each variation; or create a climax. Maybe you want to organize your piece into short sections that are seemingly disparate, but then come together at the end. However you choose to structure it, it is good to be aware that there is not only one way to do it. Make sure the organization adds to and doesn't detract from your piece.

If it works for you, then lean into it. If not, then consider some of these ways you can organize:

ORGANIZATION OF A STORY:

Narratives might be in chronological order, explaining events as they happen, with a climactic arc and some kind of resolution of a character's journey. They could also have different types of structures, telling the stories of separate characters' lives alongside each other, not necessarily in order of events, with each character taking a chapter.

ORGANIZATION OF A SONG:

Consider the traditional organization of a song. There is the verse, which is the narrative part of the song, and the chorus, which is the catchy part that keeps repeating. Then there are bridges that link together the verses and the chorus; a middle eight, which helps break up the song pattern; and perhaps a key change to heighten and build to maximum effect. Songs typically end with a coda or repetition of the chorus. How could you use this type of organization to enhance your material, whether you are creating a song, a choreography, a play, or a large arena concert? Maybe you think of your choreography as having a catchy phrase that repeats, and that's your "chorus." If that's your chorus, then what would be your middle eight?

ORGANIZATION OF AN ESSAY:

In an essay, you have an introductory paragraph stating an opinion or introducing a topic, theme, or problem. Then there is the body of paragraphs, which argue, illuminate, and clarify the key points. The concluding paragraph restates the topic and points out the larger significance of your initial argument. What if you were to write a song as though it were an essay?

ORGANIZATION OF A SURREALIST PIECE:

The Exquisite Corpse was a method invented by surrealists in which you create the next part based only on the immediately preceding section, not taking into consideration the entire product. You add to a composition in sequence either by following a rule, or by only allowing yourself to be influenced by the previous section. In this method of organization, the piece becomes almost like one nonsensical journey. It toys with the mind's desire to make meaning of the whole, and instead focuses on what's happening in the present.

ORGANIZATION OF A LIFE CYCLE:

Consider the cyclical life of a flower. Its stem pushes through the earth, it grows upwards and buds, and it finally opens into a flower. Then it withers, drops its petals and seeds, and dies, only to burst forth again in the spring. What kind of effect would this have if it were used in a song? Or a one-act play?

ORGANIZATION OF A SUITE, SYMPHONY, OR CONCERTO:

Try using sections that you repeat and intersperse in a sequence such as ABA or ABCABCA to create a sense of order, build dramatic impact, or explore one character or theme with variety.

ORGANIZATION OF A FIVE-ACT PLAY:

Act 1, which is considered the prologue, prepares the audience by introducing the characters and setting. Act 2 introduces conflict to that world. In act 3, there is rising action and climax. Then in act 4, the action falls, and finally, in act 5, we finish with denouement, where the tone and moral of the play is underscored.

SIDE NOTE:

It's really difficult to describe the key points of Articulation without imparting a set of aesthetics onto you. For example, just by mentioning that you should consider your audience, you may feel like I am infringing on your right to not give a damn about them. "You are neglecting my postmodern rights!" you might say, waving your fist in the air with the injustice. So, just keep in mind that everything is up for interpretation, reinterpretation, reinvention. Go forth and reinvent the rules if you like. It's all about making conscious choices...or not! I guess you could make unconscious choices and call that, uh, your artistic choice. But it helps to know a little bit about the ways it has been done before so you can know where to break the rules.

UNITY:

Our minds are always grasping to make meaning of something. When you give an audience disparate parts on purpose, they will still be trying to figure out how it all fits together and why you chose to put all these different things onstage in the same evening. We're always trying to make meaning of something and figure it out. We can't help it. So if you're moving toward creating chaos, create it deliberately. Or at least understand that state of grasping for the thread that you will be hurling your audience into otherwise.

CONSIDERATIONS IN CREATING UNITY:

1. Relationships: When there is more than one person onstage, then there is a relationship that should be considered and a deliberate choice to be made about how the people do or don't interact and why. They are either connected or not. If they're in worlds of their own, to what purpose is it to have them onstage at the same time? The same thing goes with instrumentation. Why a cello and a piano? Why not viola?

2. Space: Performers' placement in specific areas of the theater has been studied and used in stagecraft for hundreds of years. There are certain things you might want to consider. For example, downstage right is a powerful, focus-grabbing position. You can use an understanding of space to be most effective and powerful in your placement of people and things.

3. Time: Time reaches each of us very personally, which makes it an interesting variable. Each viewer has their own pace, rhythm, and cadence. So how can you use time, timing, the elation of time, to underscore or create unity in your work? Are you showing the arc of a character in short montages throughout their life, or are we getting a real-

time look at their life for this one hour? What effect does it have on the audience's perception of the character to see them in real time?

4. Structure: Otherwise known as organization, which is what we were just talking about. Whether you like it or not, everything you present has a beginning, middle, and an end. The audience shows up and considers that a beginning. When it is over and they go home, that is the end—and there is something in between. How can the structure and organization of your piece further clarify or unify what the piece itself is about?

5. Materials: How can physical objects, props, costuming, set pieces, and lighting further illuminate, underscore, or bring together an understanding of the piece itself? Are the material objects movable or stagnant? Flimsy or sturdy? Bright and attractive? Dark and dingy? A simple red scarf can signify a range of dramatic effects and completely change the course of a narrative.

YOUR SIGNATURE RECIPE: ESTABLISHING ARTISTIC VOICE

Artistic voice is something that develops and deepens over time. Make work or perform ten times, a hundred times, a thousand times, and you'll start to see a thread there. Artistic voice is what you do, how you do it, and why you do it, and the underlying beliefs that support that. Is there a common theme to the choices that you make, to what interests you again and again over time? That's artistic voice. No matter where you are in your career or path as a creator, you already have artistic voice. As you've read through this book, you've likely begun to identify your artistic voice based on the choices you make, your variables, the way you organize, as well as your creative process and how you like to work with Alignment and Allowing. If you haven't yet, then begin taking notes on your preferences. Becoming aware of those things you say yes to may seem like a no-brainer to you, but they are indicators of style—of voice. This section will help you understand your artistic voice so you can continue making choices to clarify it.

The Four Biggest Benefits to Clarifying Your Artistic Voice

Being Clear about Artistic Voice Will Make All Your Choices Easier

Opportunities will either be a "Hell YES!" or a "Hell NO!" to you, and you will be less likely to stretch yourself too thin or feel like you're all over the place. When I was a young dancer new to the San Francisco Bay Area, I took every dancing gig I could get my hands on. If someone asked me to dance with their company, I would seize the opportunity and do it. It was excellent research for my own artistic voice because I tried so many things and figured out what I really liked, but eventually it became draining. I had to start saying no and making clear choices.

You Get to Tell the World Who You Are

Once you are clear, then you'll be able to express that clarity to others, transmit that clear, aligned message, and have some control over how you are presented in the world. It may seem tempting to let others describe you, but it's not advisable. Look at the all the stories of famous musicians who have fought with music executives over creative control. Look at those artists who are manufactured by music corporations as an example of what the market supposedly wants. They don't last because they don't represent an authentic voice. Wouldn't you rather tell the world who you are?

It Will Give Your Audience a Way into Your Work

Having artistic voice, or a sustained interest over time, helps your audience find you and understand you, and inspires them to follow you. It's like reading a book series. They can't wait until the next part of the story is released.

Artistic Voice Lifts You Up Out of the Competition

If you know what you're about and are continually deepening and refining this, then you will exist in a category all your own and will no longer feel like you have to compete with everyone else for a spot that someone else has defined for you.

Artistic voice is *what* you do, *how* you do it, *why* you do it, and the *underlying beliefs* that support all of that. When all four of these components are aligned with one another —when your beliefs are evident in what you do and the way you do things—then your artistic voice becomes easy to understand, and you become a lighthouse for your devoted fans. You become a showstopper, people's mouths fall open when they watch you, and concert curators and bookers can't wait to get their hands on you.

Artistic Voice Is *What* You Do

Quite literally, what actions are you choosing to do? What are your variables? Are you playing a particular instrument? Are you making dance? Are you performing one-woman shows?

Artistic Voice Is *How* You Do It

In what way, with what style, with what flair, are you doing things, and what variables do you use? Are you contemporizing Persian dances using streamlined minimal lines? Are you focusing on rhythm and culture to give dancers a baseline to improvise from? Are you breaking the rules of conventional musical theatre to tell stories in a deeper way? Have you been traveling the world and soaking in the music of different folk artists in order to put it together in a new way? How are you doing the composing, playing, dancing, choreographing, singing? In what way do you tell those stories? What's your style? Playful? Generous? Deadly serious with a lot of gravitas?

These things reveal themselves by the variables you use—the paint and colors you choose to focus on, the materials that you work with as a sculptor of sound and molder of movement.

Artistic Voice Is *Why* You Do It

What drives you? What compels you onward? It usually ain't the big paycheck, so what is it? Are you in love with the connection between sound and vibration—do you get a kick out of feeling the audience ride the waves with you? Do you love watching dancers experience themselves through your work? Is there a story you can't stop telling and are you endlessly fascinated with telling it in a new way from a new angle each time? Why do you do these things?

Artistic Voice Is the *Underlying Beliefs* That Support All of the Above

Artistic voice is the beliefs that give life and artistic breath to your *what, how,* and *why.* Do you believe that there is an archetypal truth in the folk songs of the people, and that more people should hear them? Do you believe that rhythm is the key to understanding culture? Do you believe that everyone can find themselves in a story and that stories heal old wounds? Do you believe that efficiency is beautiful? Do you believe that everyone has the ability to learn to improvise?

Artistic voice is one of those things that we know when we see it, am I right? When someone has a distinct or defined artistic style, they stand out. We feel such a genuine emanation of wholeness and clarity from them that we want to follow them everywhere. Can you remember the last time you felt that way about someone you saw perform? Where you just practically wanted to follow them home and be their best friend, you were so enthralled with them? This is the power of artistic voice.

AN EXAMPLE OF ARTISTIC VOICE

In 1999, I was a TV host for the Edinburgh Arts Festival Revue. Each day, I'd go into hair and makeup for the show and be given a list of artists I was presenting that day (some of whom I had the pleasure of recruiting to be there). When I walked out onto the stage, I got to pretend I was David Letterman or Johnny Carson introducing the artists and telling the audience what was so great about them. It was a blast! My favorite moments were chatting with the artists backstage prior to their performances and finding some detail I could include in the introduction that would make them memorable to the TV audience. One of the moments that stands out in my mind from that time was interviewing an eleven-year-old girl who was so incredibly composed onstage and off. She was there with her handler, but answered all her own questions in polite but short sentences, not wasting a single word. She was dressed all in white, and her white-blond hair was cut in a short, blunt bob.

When she got into her position onstage in front of the microphone, she didn't wiggle or look around like most eleven-year-olds might do. She didn't move a muscle until it was her cue to sing. And then her mouth dropped open and an incredible piercing beautiful sound rang out against the backdrop of electronic music. It was one of the most riveting things I had ever seen. When I later asked this little girl if she was having fun singing onstage, she looked serious and said,

"I like the one note. I like to perfect that one note."

Now let's ignore for a moment how incredible it was to hear a young girl speak with such gravitas. It was a little awe inspiring, I can tell you. I mean, she was Finnish, so it could have been due to the language barrier, I don't know, but it doesn't matter. What amazes me to think of it now is the fact that *why she did it* (because it was so simple, and for her that was her kind of fun) was evident in both *what she did* (she sang very simple notes over electronic music) and *how she did it* (with her simple robe, simple, clean hairstyle, and no extra movement). So all the components of artistic voice were fully aligned, which made her artistic voice not only genuine, but clear and recognizable to all who watched her.

Maker's Perspective

There is only ever one perspective you can make a work from. There is only one person's opinion you can ever really please. There is one lens through which you can view your work and it should be fiercely and unabashedly your own. A good piece is focused. If you keep switching your lens between what you like and what you are guessing others might think or feel, your piece will come out feeling dispersed and scattered.

You won't be building toward artistic voice, either. Make your piece to suit your tastes. Please yourself, and your work will come across as focused, vibrant, strong, unified. Yeah, it could piss some people off, but that is what our work sometimes does. The world is diverse. You are aligned with your vision. If you diffuse that with others' ideas, or worse, with your idea of what their opinions might be, then you say nothing with your work. When you keep your perspective focused and stay true to your artistic voice, you'll become a beacon of light that shines out in every direction and attracts your audience, your collaborators, and your success.

Defining the Weird Little Rules of Your Universe

When I'm in the process of translating something from out of the ether and into this physical world for an audience, I often find myself with very strong opinions about what makes sense and what doesn't. These become the weird little rules of my universe. Often these rules don't make sense in the real world, but they do in the realm I have created.

Composition, to me, is making up the weird little rules of your universe and sticking to them with integrity. Even if what you're doing isn't narrative, there are always themes and patterns that can be beautifully emphasized or horribly scattered. Composition is problem solving at its finest. You are working with not only the reality of staging, space, logistics, different dancers' capabilities, and so on, but also the rules of the world you are creating. And it's important to have some rules, because they are what provides clarity. They are what makes something powerful enough to convince the audience to go along with you and suspend disbelief, so that hopefully, in the end, there is the payoff—they can *get* it. Even if only on a visceral level, they can walk away with the message, the feeling, the emotional transmission.

For example, in the weird little world I created for *The Outlaw,* cowgirls get lost in the desert and are transformed into birds of prey and then into molecules of light. At one point while making the dance, I knew I had to transition somehow from birds to molecules, but didn't know how that was going to happen. I had to root around a little.

I went back to the exploration part of art making: I considered my variables and my movement vocabulary. It finally all clicked into place when I had the birds all of a sudden pull out their guns and hold each other in a Mexican standoff. Now, normally birds don't pull out guns, but this worked because it followed the weird little rules of my universe. I had already introduced cowgirls in the dance, so since cowgirls would have guns, it worked. Now, if my birds pulled out ice cream cones it would be a different thing altogether—it would have broken my weird little rules. If my birds pulled out ice cream cones, then at that point my audience would be trying to make a connection between cowgirls, birds, and ice cream cones. Bordering tediously on the bizarre, I could have lost the audience. When things stretch outside of the weird little world you've created, then the audience stops caring. There is a hole in the suspension of disbelief.

TIPS FOR CREATING THE WEIRD LITTLE RULES OF YOUR UNIVERSE

Here are some things I think about while crafting my own weird little rules. Naturally, if you are not someone who crafts with a narrative line in your work, then some of these won't apply, but regardless, they can be a good starting point for things to consider:

1. **Name Things**

   As soon as I get a good whiff of something that excites me enough to run with it, I try to give it a title. It may not end up being the actual title, but it is like a shorthand. I often find it introduces imagery and ideas that help me begin to form my universe. When I first started crafting *The Outlaw,* I was simply referring to it as a "cowgirls" section and a "birds" section. This helped clarify some intention and gave us tons of images and movement to work with, but when I found the word *outlaw,* then the piece started to really flesh out. It simultaneously encompassed all sections and created a focus that wasn't there before.

2. **Identify Hunger**

   What do your characters/musicians/actors/dancers desire? What is their urgent need? Get clear about their purpose for their action.

3. **Identify Conflict**

   Is there an underlying desire that is in opposition to the first desire you listed? In *The Outlaw,* the characters the dancers portrayed were wary of other people. They wanted to stand their ground, to kick some ass, but underneath that there was a deeper desire to belong, to be a part of something. Now, when it came time for my dancers to dance the piece, I didn't ask them to concentrate on both desires, but it was helpful to me as a choreographer to understand them in order to shape the arc of the piece.

4. **Reflect These Things through Composition**

   How can the desires be highlighted in the choreography? In *The Outlaw,* the dancers were dancing very individualistically throughout most of the piece until the end, when they came together and danced in unison. This satisfied the deeper desire of the characters to belong. How does the way in which the dancers are moving underscore the themes of the piece? If I'm working with cowgirls, then I'm wanting strong, clear, hard footwork, and simple attacking movements.

5. Determine the Focus

Where is the performer's focus supposed to be? Out at the audience, internal, at the floor, on other dancers? Where on other dancers? Why?

6. Trim the Fat

What is extraneous? Where is the fat to be trimmed? You can make a million choices, but one big extraneous thing can block your beautiful crafting from view and muddle everything. For example, say I've choreographed a simple and elegant moment with one dancer. If I'm smart, I won't distract from it with squawking or big movements of birds behind it. It's a good rule to always ask, "Is there anything we can do without?" Even when editing, it's still important to remember that creativity is moving toward something, not away from it. Even as you are taking things away (and, in a sense, saying no to them), you want to be fixed on that act in service of the vision of the thing you are moving toward. It's more productive to keep your focus on what you're refining instead of what's not working.

7. Give Your Audience Gesture Doorways

Are there key gestures that feel purposeful and meaningful? Are they clear? Are they memorable? Gestures, commonly understood movements of the body that signal something, are things that people remember. Gestures are the things that connect the superhuman grandiose dancer on the stage to the everyday audience member sitting in the seat. Gestures provide a doorway into your work. Gestures are familiar and so they are memorable. The same effect can be seen in music in the form of familiar hooks, jingles, well-known melodies, or sound effects. They are how we, as social animals, communicate with each other every day. They speak volumes.

8. Clarify All Intention

Are the dancers clear about what is going on? Are there ever places in the piece where it becomes unclear where the focus should be? Where are they moving to next? What are they longing for? The director/composer/choreographer should have a clear idea of where the focus should be at any moment and be sure that it's communicated to the people onstage.

9. Be Aware of Momentum

Are there ever places where the energy drops? These are usually parts that have been glossed over or imagined as improvised, but not thoroughly thought out.

10. Identify the Audience's Hunger

What will the audience be hungry for? If you have a group scene of chaos, then after a few minutes your audience will be craving unity, peace, or at least some kind of resolution. It's your choice if you give them that satisfaction or not. But it is a good idea to have a feeling for what emotion wants to take over at any given moment.

11. Consider Surprises

Once you get more and more clear about what your weird little rules are, then it is fun to consider breaking them. You can change or challenge the themes so that the work doesn't become too homogenous or too predictable. For example, once I've established that my outlaws are tough, I start to consider, can they also be delicate? Vulnerable? Fearful? How could you insert an element of surprise by breaking a rule and still have it translate cohesively? Whether you make the choice to insert a surprise or not, it is worth considering some options.

This is composition, and it's the part that can really feel more like the labor of birthing the piece. It feels hugely important, and it is important, because it is where the creation gets distilled, translated, articulated into something that will be satisfying and clear to witnesses. Exercising your preferences is where you discover and uncover the weird little rules of the universe you're creating.

If Alignment is the loner and Allowing is the social butterfly, then Articulation is the bossypants leader people are excited to follow: finally firmly out in the world, getting it done, at the helm, in charge, dynamic. Articulation is saying, "This is my universe, and here are the rules!"

ESTABLISHING YOUR CREATIVE PROCESS: A NOTE ABOUT LEARNING HOW TO COOK

So, what makes a good cook? Someone who cooks! The same goes with Articulation. The more you practice, the clearer your articulation becomes, the more efficiently you make your point, and the more elegant your creation comes across. And you can make more and more of that type of thing that just gets better and better. This is why Prince wrote so many awesome songs as one of the most prolific songwriters of our time. One of Prince's biggest gifts was merging lyrics with music so that they were in acute alignment with one another. The result was a powerful song. He figured out how to do this, and by expanding on it and continuing to focus on that gift, he just kept getting better at it. He was a smart guy, Prince.

Anytime I've set out to do a new type of creative thing, whether it's making a dance with a new group of dancers, recording a meditation album, or even writing this book, I'm struck by the fact that when I try a new thing, I spend a lot of time figuring out the process of how to make that new type of thing.

For example, in trying to figure out how to record my meditation album *Tuning the Creative Mind*, I had to experiment and learn how best to record it. Would I improvise the words or write a script beforehand? How tightly did I want to structure the arc of the meditation? What was the best pace to speak in? And did I want to record my own music or use GarageBand tracks?

There were a million variables that I had never had to face before, because this was my first time doing this particular thing. I think we have to give ourselves a break anytime we attempt something that is creatively totally new to us. Maybe you have always written novels, and now you're doing short stories and are struggling a bit. Maybe you are a classical musician who has always focused on playing Mozart, and now you are embarking on original compositions. Learning how to do that, the exact creative process, takes some figuring out. So go easy. Just because you know how to make salad doesn't mean you know how to bake. It takes practice.

There isn't a total right way to do any of this. Some of us know exactly what we are making in the kitchen and assemble our ingredients beforehand. Others just see what we have in the fridge and figure it out as we are throwing the food together. Do whatever works for you. If you like to organize and create an outline first before you ever start to develop the raw material, then do that. If you're more of a trial-and-error person, then that's fine too.

I know I put these sections inside the Articulation chapter as though I could give you the exact step-by-step directions in order to create something, as though it's linear and easy. Ha! It's not. Articulation can be wild and messy, and it can feel like rooting around in the dark. But this is the fun of it because at some point, you find the light switch and everything comes into clear view. So enjoy the groping around blindly. Trust it. It's part of the game.

BAKING THE PIE TO PERFECTION: THE FINAL TOUCHES

IDENTIFY A GAME CHANGER

I find that asking ourselves to focus on everything at once ends up with the same result as focusing on, or trying to fix, nothing at all. This is why I often like to use the concept of a game changer. When you are looking at a final piece, knowing it isn't quite polished yet, but not sure what thing to address, you must ask yourself: What is the game changer in this scenario? What is the one thing that, if I focused on it, would have the potential to exponentially shift everything else? If I could only master or fix one thing right now, which thing would make the biggest difference?

When I was rehearsing *The Outlaw*, the dancers and I had used recorded music. Two weeks before we went up, we began using the live musicians we would actually have in performance. This happens all the time in theatre unless you are a funded ballet company or have full-time musicians at your disposal somehow otherwise. It's just too expensive to have live musicians in all of your rehearsals, so there is sometimes this awkward period when you first bring the musicians in where it feels like the whole thing will fall apart.

For *The Outlaw*, the game changer was finding a way to have the music soar at the end. Limited by instrumentation, I had to rework the choreography and piece in order to create the crescendo with movement instead of solely relying on sound. Out of all the things I could have worked on, this felt like the most important—because without it, the energy of the entire piece would have fallen flat at the end.

The game changer keeps you from over-tweaking. Don't be a tweaker. Have faith in the ingredients and the process.

HOW DO I KNOW WHEN IT'S DONE?

Overcooking can ruin all the best ingredients. How do you know when you are finished? Look for the golden outside. Notice when the scent of it begins take over the whole house in a cloud of deliciousness. Bake a few. Burn a few. Learn the smell of the moments right before it burns.

How do you smell it burning? Irritability. Other people you are working with start giving you silent looks and get quiet when you come into the room. Confusion means it probably isn't done yet, and enthusiasm and eagerness? Well, look. Nothing's every really going to be done perfectly; but, if you get enthusiasm and eagerness from those around you, then that's the indication that everything has come to full circle, and your vision is in alignment with you and the people performing it.

ARTICULATION
SELF-ASSESSMENT QUESTIONS

✓ Did I give myself the opportunity to step back and allow, to generate new ideas in the middle of this process, or did I plow right through, forcing myself to work on one idea?

✓ If I had to sum up my main objective or the one big thing I wanted to get across in this piece, can I look at all the different aspects (lighting, costume, script, score, color scheme, organization of space, organization of narrative) and say that they support that?

✓ If there are pieces that don't, then were they deliberate?

✓ Is *what* I'm doing supported by *how* and *why* I'm doing it?

✓ Is there any place where the energy drops or the actors/dancers/musicians seem unfocused or unnecessarily tense?

✓ Are there any compromises in this piece that I don't stand behind? Suggestions from others that don't feel 100 percent authentic to me?

✓ Is there any place in this piece that is redundant?

✓ Am I assuming my audience is smart? Or am I spoon-feeding them and leaving little to be imagined?

✓ Am I violating any of the rules of my weird little universe?

✓ Is there another way this could be organized that would be more effective?

SEGUE QUESTION

✓ What would I like to try next?

CREATIVITY IS MOVING TOWARD SOMETHING, NOT AWAY FROM IT

I have a friend who is a writer. She writes and writes and although she is extremely good at it, and has published her short stories, she has never finished any of her novels. She's written many drafts. I've read them; they're fantastic. She has gotten very close to finishing, but she stops at the same point in the process every time. What she tells me is always something like this:

> "Well, I recognize now that this particular plot line has
> to resolve in an elegant way, but I don't know what that is
> so I just can't bring myself to write it."

What I tell her, and what I long to tell you, is that any motion forward is better than none at all. I know that if she takes any step toward writing that bridge in her novel, she will begin to figure it out. Even if she starts with a lousy solution, other ideas will begin to show up as she continues to write. The answers are in the movement forward.

> Anytime you are having trouble with Articulation,
> it is because you've basically stopped playing the game.

You've shifted your mind so heavily into work mode instead of play mode. The Creative Formula isn't a straight linear path. There always needs to be a dance among the three parts. If you find yourself overwhelmed, confused, or stuck, then it's time to go back to Alignment, or maybe time to take a wider perspective and do some Allowing. Whatever you do, keep yourself moving forward and don't ever forget that it's all just a game.

If there is one thing you can take away from this book besides an understanding of Alignment, Allowing, and Articulation, it's this:

Yes, the Creative Formula is serious important business that
deserves your full integrity and attention, but also, lighten up!

We can't get to the best, juiciest ideas if we're too serious. We too often get
in our own way and when we say we are creating, what we are really doing is
scowling at the Facebook posts of our peers who seem to be doing better than
us. We begin to question ourselves: "Who do I think I am to attempt this?"

Lighten up. This isn't life or death. This is creative stuff: Making shows.
Adding value to the world. Making people think. Being evocative. Fun stuff.
All the stuff you used to do when you were little and dressed up your little
sister in your mom's kitchen apron to perform *Giselle* in the living room. So,
as I used to tell my dance students:

Don't take yourself seriously, but do it with integrity.
Show up.
Play the game.
Then, win or lose,
go home and treat yourself to a nice dinner.

Step 4: I'm Done. Now What?

So, that's finished! Phew! ...Um, now what? A frequent problem that performers and creators come to me with is keeping momentum. I know professionals who are brilliant at making one piece, but experience a terrible depression afterward that they have to drag themselves out of before making anything else again. Make space for fear by taking time off, and it can sometimes creep in. But I also know very successful and prolific professionals who have figured out how to keep their momentum and survive the dips from one project to the next.

How to Keep Momentum from One Project to the Next

If you're someone who has trouble getting started in the first place, then there are a few things to consider before you're done with this project that will help catapult you into the next one without dipping too far into a lull. It takes tremendous energy to pull yourself up and get started all over again. Here are my suggestions:

Always book at least four gigs out.

My friend James Boblak is a recording engineer, and he's seen hundreds of musicians pass through his studio at various levels of success in their careers.

97

When I asked him what his advice would be to artists, he recommended always booking at least four gigs ahead. It's an external motivator, but one that works. Always know what your next show is going to be. Always be setting up more. Better yet, plan out your year. Look at a calendar and start booking/inquiring/applying for festivals, concerts, and tours eighteen months in advance. Keep them on a regular calendar so next year is even easier.

> Plan your Exhales (performances, shows, exhibits) around
> the times of the year when you personally tend to have the
> desire to be more extroverted and energetic.

> Plan your Inhales (study, professional development, creation,
> collaboration) around times when you know yourself to turn inward.

Personally, I find the energy of the seasons tends to inform what I naturally feel inclined to do: spring is an exceptional time for me to create; fall is excellent for launching a new project or teaching a course; December, January, and February are for writing, daydreaming, and planning; and summer months are for playing, vacations, or more whimsical and improvisational performances. By knowing this now and planning for it, I'm able to keep my momentum while transferring it to the parts of myself needing to be nourished or expressed.

> Always be asking, "What's next?"

What helps me finish the current project is thinking about the next one. Honestly, I always have multiple projects I'm working on at various stages. I don't try to make them all happen at once, but I do keep many projects on the back burner. It's the same theory as Benjamin Franklin's Lazy Susan, which I mentioned in "Divide and Conquer." I always have incredible ideas for something when I'm not focused on it and hence not pressured, so I've set myself up to expect this and plan for it. I always start creating a folder for something the minute I know it's a potential project. As I have ideas about it, I jot them down in my notebook and then later I rip that page out and put it in the right folder for that future project. Then, guess what? When my current project is over I have a folder full of notes, already getting me well on my way with the next one.

Try creating art in a series.

Whenever possible, I suggest that artists consider making art in a series as opposed to doing ad hoc projects. There are several reasons for this:

1. Having figured out the process for one part of the series, you conserve energy by being able to focus more on the deepening and exploration of the subject, as opposed to re-creating the wheel each time. This is akin to learning a new recipe. If you've always made cold salads, but now you want to bake cakes, then you have to learn all about the process of cake making. Once the energy of learning to sift flour and measure accurately is taken care of, and then the energy can go into playing with different recipes and making small adjustments and variations.

2. Making art in a series is the best way to get to your best work—you are less pressured about something and more free. You are able to be more allowing when you have multiple pieces, as opposed to the pressure of one important piece.

3. Making art in a series is also great because it generates momentum. Having one subject to explore gives you new questions and viewpoints to explore it from. It's a constant unfolding of a subject that you can ride for a very long time.

KNOW WHEN TO REALIGN

Momentum is a buzzword right now, and I totally get why. Sometimes the toughest part of making anything is just getting started. So why not avoid that altogether, get started once, and then ride the wave of momentum forevermore? I'm all for it. But I do think there are some of us who need a flat-out break. If you find your life falling apart, if you feel disconnected from your family or your friends, if you find yourself turning to drugs or alcohol on a regular basis, if you don't sleep on a regular schedule, but you do cry on one, then you should take a break. Stop the momentum. Go back to Alignment. There's no reason to continue a spiral when it's a downward one. You really do need a reset and it's ok. You got going once; you can do it again.

UNDERSTAND THE DIP

Anytime I end a workshop intensive or I'm working with a performer who has just finished a run of performances, I advise them to take extra good gentle care of themselves. And then I wait for the inevitable call or email where they explain to me how low or depressed they feel as they return to a life that is less glamorous, and where they have to deal with laundry and paying bills. There is this thing that happens, this awesome suspension of "everyday," that we as artists, creators, performers get to experience.

It is an exceptional life to lead, it's hella fun, and we wonder why everyone else doesn't want to do it too. The hyperawareness and attunement that happen as we play in this special and magical world we've create can be awesome in the truest sense of the word. We are incredibly lucky. And coming back down to earth after that can be hard.

What is really happening is that we have expanded spiritually. A part of us, in these extremely focused states of Alignment, Allowing, and Articulation, has evolved. The rest of the people in our lives—family members, coworkers—just don't seem to get it. A weekend of performances with all of the emotional and spiritual journey involved is tough to explain to someone who spent their weekend getting their car serviced and watching the game on TV. It's tough for them to relate to the artistic evolutions that are not necessarily the same as most people's everyday evolutions. They still treat us like we're trudging along like everyone else. We want to yell at them,

"I've tasted something exceptional and I am different now! And I know this, so just accept it!"

Our being has expanded, but real life will take a while to catch up. This leaves a gap that you can fall into. It's a hazardous trench with a long fall and a painful landing—though it does not end in death, just painful bruises. But it's scary on the way down, so look out for it. Go slowly after your show run/transformational workshop/exhibit and be gentle with yourself. Eat something. Regroup. Reread the "Inhalation and Exhalation" section of this book under "Alignment." You just did a big exhalation. It's OK to be quiet and inhale for a while.

No, people will not forget you if you stay off social media for a few weeks. Yes, all those glorious shifts in consciousness really did happen.

Nothing is lost. You are not dying. You are not depressed. You are just supposed to be with your friends and pay attention to your family and practice radical self-care. When you're bored as shit, you'll go back and clean out your artist brushes and get back into your studio for the next masterpiece.

THE CREATIVE FORMULA
IN THE STUDIO

As I mentioned before, the Creative Formula originated out of my own studio work, when I'd show up in a bare room with mirrors wanting to get the most out of my time there. It's an extremely effective way to organize a session of creative or technical work. Consciously using all the ingredients, from Alignment to Allowing to Articulation, sets you up for the most inspired and fully present composition or practice session.

When we are working on our own, it can help to have a system in place. Notice I didn't say a routine! The Creative Formula can be used as a road map, but not necessarily as a routine, because its success depends on staying in tune with how you feel at any moment. In order to get the most out of the Creative Formula, you want to always allow your emotions to guide you. Using the self-assessment questions at the end of each chapter is also a great way to do this. There is nothing wrong with forming habits that work for you as far as getting yourself warmed up and ready, but I would strongly suggest when using the Creative Formula that you continue to be fully present to your emotions—to notice when you become bored with a particular warm-up, for example, or when a certain type of improvisation leaves you uninterested. This is a sign to move on, to freshen up your approach and try something new.

Although I described the Creative Formula in this book as being laid out in a sequential manner (that is, first you Align, then you Allow, then you Articulate), I want to emphasize that they are not meant to always go in one linear direction.

The Creative Formula is *flexible*! And the parts, Alignment, Allowing, and Articulation, should be treated as necessary ingredients, not an itinerary. When you are in the beginning of creating a work, you will need to do a lot of allowing—a lot of opening up of possibility and playing around. Eventually things will start to click into place and you'll begin articulating. But it would be a mistake to let you think it ends there, because that's when you really begin to dance between articulation and allowing. When you find yourself stuck in the articulation process, sometimes you will need to step back into the Allowing phase and ask yourself questions like, "What am I still interested in here?" and "What is actually working?" When you're in the Articulation phase, you still need to be flexible enough to go back and allow, using it as a tool to pivot when needed.

READY TO WORK—ALIGN BEFORE YOU'RE IN THE STUDIO

There is nothing lonelier than being in a bare room on your own with the pressure to make work and no desire to do it, which is why I highly suggest finding alignment before you ever step foot in the studio. This could mean scheduling your solo studio time right after a technique class so your body is warm and responsive, or going for an outdoor run to get the body flowing before the studio, or listening to music on your headphones or in your car on the way to a session to get you in the zone. Another favorite way to align for me is to watch videos of some of my favorite dancers. This inhalation of inspiration gets me in touch with why I love to make dance and makes me juiced to get down to working on it.

If you are working with actors, dancers, or musicians in the studio, then make sure you take the time to warm them up properly. Even though professionals should know enough to come early and warm up on their own, you can still spend a few minutes taking the group through a warm-up together. There is a unification and a cohesion that happens when you do this, and the ten or fifteen minutes you spend doing this is earned back in the intense productivity that follows a good group warm-up.

QUICK TIPS FOR ARTICULATING IN THE STUDIO

TO CREATE UNIFICATION:

Repeat what you know. For example, run your dance from the beginning to wherever you've left off in the middle to get inside the piece again and allow more of the piece to come. This is important when you are wanting to feel for the logical progression of what wants to come forward.

TO CREATE DIVERSITY:

Don't start with the dance itself. Make something completely different. Perhaps pick out a completely different piece of music. Work out some phrases to this and then try working that into the piece. How much of the contrast can you continue to leave in? What kinds of textures does this add? How does this new piece add new insight to your existing material? Have you dropped the thread, or can you still feel the continuation of the original theme?

TO EVALUATE WITH A FRESH EYE:

Familiarity is mind numbing. Our minds have evolved to perceive change because change is threatening to our existence. We are hardwired to notice change and relax when there isn't any. So when there is no change, our minds can fall into a sort of status quo, a peaceful relationship with whatever we're surrounded by, a comfortable stasis. If you're wanting to really evaluate a piece you are working on with a fresher eye, then you'll need to alter it to open your mind to it again. You can do this in many different ways:

Put your work on someone else: If you're creating a piece on yourself, teach it to someone else and observe it through them. Even if they don't have time to learn it correctly or practice it to perfection, there is something in the relay of information that sheds new light on something, as well as watching the way the material works or doesn't on someone else. You might catch awkward transitions when they're executed by a musician that has a lesser skill level, benefiting you differently than when you had a virtuoso player glossing through it. Or you might recognize that you haven't created a sufficient relationship between characters that you hadn't noticed before due to the natural chemistry of your original actors.

Change the music: If you're creating choreography, then try the combinations to a new piece of music. I find this is especially helpful in pointing out transitions that need work. A good transition should work regardless of accompaniment. Also, without even meaning to, our bodies respond differently to different music, so changing it up can also open opportunities for different textures that might be interesting to integrate.

Change the instrumentation, seating, spacing, audience orientation: This same rule applies to just about anything you can think to change. Make people play next to each other who never usually do. Change where the audience is in relation to the actors. Pretend the audience is in the rafters, or in the round. The idea isn't that you will keep these changes, just that it will open up new possibilities. It can be extremely useful to highlight problems you might not have noticed before.

In the Studio
Self-Assessment Questions

✓ Do I leave myself something to work on for the next session before I leave?

✓ Do I look forward to my time in the studio?

✓ Do I use my preferences of working alone or with others to the fullest advantage? (For example, am I doing the work I need to do to prepare to work with someone else? Do I notice when bringing another person into my studio might be helpful to give me a fresh perspective or fresh energy to a project?)

The Creative Formula
in the Classroom, Groups, or Workshops

CARMEN

Twelve-year-old Carmen moves as though underwater and her head looks disconnected from her body, like it's resisting the dance. Her limbs are moving to the correct technical positions, but it feels like they are being placed there, not reaching for the edges of space. She keeps glancing over at me, but surreptitiously, as though hoping I won't notice. I look around at the faces of all the girls—we have worked all week building trust as a group to get to this point—and they seem a little bored. Carmen is a favorite, and, being younger, a bit of a darling of the group, but it's clear from their expressions that this is the dance they are used to seeing from Carmen. Then a memory floats up in my mind vividly: Carmen, on the first day of this workshop, when we were sharing in a group after the writing exercise.

"Carmen, stop for a moment," I say gently. She pauses and drops her limbs like a puppet with the strings let go and stands looking at me, a slightly worried expression of anticipation on her sweet, round face.

"What was it that you said that you wanted on the first day?" I prompt her.

"That, um, I want to be a good dancer?" The question in her voice lingers in the air for a moment. I let it.

"You said," I gather clarity as I talk, the notes I had taken earlier in the week seared in my mind, "you said that you wanted to show everyone what a great dancer you are and that you aren't just a good girl." She nods.

"So, Carmen. What happens if you aren't a good girl?" I ask.

"Umm...." She isn't sure what I'm asking.

"What are you afraid will happen if you aren't a good girl?"

She ponders this and really thinks for a moment. The length of time she takes to do this feels really good. Already I can feel some part of her wanting to take up a little more space.

"If I'm not good, then people might not like me," she finally answers.

"Hmm." I nod and make a soft sound of compassion. I let this answer and the weight of it hang in the air for a moment. I look around at the room and say to the older girls, "If she was bad sometimes, would you still like Carmen?" I ask.

"Yeah!" they respond, nodding their heads supportively.

"Wouldn't you love to see her be a little bad?"

"Yes!" They are right there with me, these girls.

I look at Carmen with a grin. "OK, Carmen. Look around at all your friends. Look into their faces and really allow yourself to see what they're reflecting back to you. OK, good. So, I want you to dance this piece again, but this time, I want you to be bad. However you want. Be naughty and wild and mean and whatever else you think is bad, OK?"

I turn on the music and she begins dancing. Just like before, only it appears she may have inched back to hide into herself even a touch further.

"OK, nanny nanny blah blah bpffffft!" I jump up and start wagging around like I'm sassing her, making fart noises and bad faces. "Make a mean face!" I say. She continues dancing with careful limbs but throws in a little wag here or there. "There you go! Even more!" I say, and then I motion to the other girls in the group to get up and now we are all sassy and wagging our butts and making funny bad-girl poses at her. It's hilarious and there's some time when it's clear it could dissolve into giggles, but I hold my focus strong.

"Come on, Carmen! In my face! Get in my face!" This continues for a while, until all of a sudden I see this flash of anger in her eyes and she comes at me in the middle of her arabesque, her face flying towards me.

She shouts, from deep in her gut, "HA!" There is a crackle in the air and I feel like I could almost see the electricity of that "Ha!" linger in the space in front of me. The other girls are stunned and delighted.

"Yes! Yes! Again!" I encourage her. She has experienced a new side of herself and I don't want her shrinking back now.

"Ha! HA! HAAAA!" she shouts as she flies around the room, her body and movements huge and full and alive with new power. This is Carmen fully expressed.

I let her finish her dance like this and then I let the group give her hugs and reflect back to her how beautiful this was. I can feel that something has changed for her forever. The people-pleaser inside of her that lets her be pushed around is no longer running the show. The fierce part has shown up. She hugs me with abandon and smiles a big smile—still sweet, still Carmen— but she walks with a new authoritative air out of the studio and into the world.

I had been using the Creative Formula only for myself for a few years before I started structuring entire workshops around it. That's when I began to see its true power and charms. It's one thing to have a secret method you use yourself, and another thing entirely to see it working for others. After seeing how well it worked once, I made the decision not only to use it as the skeleton for all of the work I did in groups, but also to share the process and wisdom of it with the participants. Still, to this day, if you came to a workshop, you would probably find me starting the day off by writing "Alignment, Allowing, and Articulation" on a whiteboard at the front of the room while describing what students can expect from the day's work.

Share the Process

While it's not wholly necessary, I recommend sharing the Creative Formula with groups you are using it with. I feel like this not only empowers people by pointing out and reflecting on the mental aspect of the creative work, but it also builds trust. People trust leaders who believe in them and practice transparency in their thoughts and plans. When you share the Creative Formula strategy out in the open, it says to them, "This is the work I'm asking you to do, and I'm trusting you to learn about it so you can listen to yourself and help me guide you."

That way, if they don't feel like doing the work, they can reflect and self-regulate. If someone in your group gets stuck, then they might realize it is a matter of going back into the Alignment phase, and that is all. By sharing the Creative Formula, you are one step closer to eliminating that "Something is wrong with me, why can't I do this?" mentality, and you can turn it into self-awareness. When others in the group are in the Allowing phase and putting pressure on themselves to make something "good," then you can help them recognize that they are heading into Articulation too soon. If you've shared the Creative Formula strategy with them, then they'll understand immediately: "Oh right, I don't need to do that yet. That comes later." If they've become stuck in Articulation, you can make them aware that there is always the option to shift to Allowing for a moment and ask them to consider self-assessment questions like, "OK, what is still interesting to me here?" By sharing the Creative Formula with them, the work will continue to work for them after you are no longer there and they will trust you even more because you've empowered them.

The Resources of the Group

The biggest reason that the Creative Formula works so well in workshops, classrooms, or any kind of group is that there is exponential value in using the people in the group to support each other, rather than hanging it all directly on the facilitator, teacher, director, or coach. Encouraging the group to support one another not only spreads out the responsibility in the room, but it also serves directly in shifting the mental awareness used in creativity.

REDIRECTION OF SELF-CONSCIOUSNESS

When doing creative work, there is a tendency to get lost inside oneself, to feel self-conscious. By using the other people in the group to support one another, the person leading the group can direct people's focus outward. By directing participants' attention to someone outside of themselves, they are shifting any self-consciousness to being conscious of the person in front of them, and hopefully connecting with another human being, which is inherently soothing and creatively generative. It can be easy to appreciate and feel good about other people once we connect with them, and so it makes getting into alignment that much easier. Once we are connected and feeling appreciative of others, then it is much easier to extend that goodwill toward ourselves as well.

CREATING A SAFE CONTAINER

When asking people to dive into their creativity, to be free, to take risks and try out new things, it's extremely important to create an atmosphere conducive to that. I find that if I take care of the following five aspects within a workshop, then the willingness of the participants increases, and they get a deeper value out of their time:

Time: In my work with people, I am known for being on time. I begin on time and I end on time and I try not to waste people's time in between. I find that when I do this effectively, then not only do people show up on time for me, but also a trust is built. Participants are able to relax more into a challenging exercise because they know that there is an end in sight. If they are doing something new and uncomfortable, then they know that it won't last forever.

Space: Take consideration of the space you will be using for the workshop. Is it huge and dwarfing? If it is, are there ways or places to organize or concentrate energy, or to utilize that space in totality? Is it noisy? Are there other people using the space at the same time? Passing by and looking in windows? I've been known to go around and shut all the windows and doors when we're about to do an intensely focused exercise, or one that takes a lot of trust. Creating a safe and comforting space can really help the atmosphere of group work.

Events: People like to know what's going on and what's going to happen next. You don't want to overwhelm people with too much information, but you also want to keep them informed of what's going on. When I begin a workshop, for example, I always give a very general overview of how the day is going to go and try to mention things that might affect their self-care (for example, expectations about bathroom and lunch breaks, and what equipment or shoes they might need). But then, when I'm in the middle of teaching, I typically will only give them one step of the exercise at a time. If they need to create eight counts of rhythm, then I only give them instructions enough to do that one piece. I don't tell them that then they'll have to make it travel across the room or whatever. I give them only the one piece of the exercise to keep them focused on the task at hand.

The Leader: No matter if everyone in the group already knows who I am, I always begin any workshop or class by sharing for a minute or two about myself and why I'm qualified to be leading them in that particular workshop. This is called positioning. If we are creating an atmosphere of trust in every area, then it's just as vital to include ourselves in it. We need to let the group know why they can trust us. They need to understand our expertise as well as why we care deeply about what we are teaching. Too often this piece is skipped and leaders try to move forward without the buy-in of the group. It's imperative to build rapport, and letting them know why you're in charge is a big piece of that.

The Participants and Group Dynamics: It's important to include exercises helping people get to know each other before diving into the real risk-taking creative activities. It's part of Alignment. I've found that even with artists who have a high level of creativity and lots of experience taking risks in front of others, it still never hurts to start with simple partner or small group exercises—the simpler, the better. Have everyone choose a partner and engage in a simple mirroring activity. Perhaps your singers can sing one note and mirror it back to each other, then slowly add more and more notes, gradually creating a call and response between them. Or perhaps, even more simply, they each tell the other one thing that they love most about the feeling of singing.

Build Trust First

Notice how people are relating to each other. I once had a group do an eye-gazing exercise, and one woman's partner simply closed her eyes. For whatever reason, she felt unable or afraid to look deeply into someone's eyes. And actually, this isn't that uncommon. Sadly, we don't spend a lot of time looking straight into people's eyes, despite how calming to the nervous system it can be. When asked to do this, people will often giggle at first, unused to the intimacy of it. So when this woman shut her eyes, I tried a few different things.

First, I gently reminded the group of the instructions, and then I moved closer to that particular couple in case the instructions hadn't been heard the first time or there was a language or hearing barrier. After I repeated the instructions, her eyes fluttered open and fixed guardedly on the woman across from her for a moment, and then squeezed tight again. There was lot of resistance there. The rest of the room was doing the exercise, but there was a lot of fidgeting and giggling. I sensed the timing wasn't quite right to dive into an all-out eye-gazing activity like this, so I simply redirected the group to a different activity.

Creative work can be a big leap of faith for many people. Depending on their level of comfort with the creative space and what type of group you are working with, there will be different levels of willingness and resistance. For example, contemporary dancers tend to be very open, receptive, and willing.

Adolescents who've never taken an acting or dance class might not be as open at first. Middle-aged businessmen probably will take a longer warm-up. Every group will be different, and there will be differences within the group to notice as well. Not everyone in the group will be able or willing to come along with whatever exercise you give them. It is important not to pander too much to the most resistant participants. Oftentimes, if there are a handful of people in the room who are really playing the game and letting the exercises work through them, they can shift the energy of the room as the more resistant are inspired and swept up in the fun.

While it's important not to focus too much on the most resistant person in the room, you also don't want to completely ignore them either, as sometimes the most vocal or obvious person's reaction can actually be a barometer for how the more compliant participants are feeling as well. Some people will suffer inside silently or go about their work diligently, but with forced smiles. Those are as much of a sign of resistance as shutting one's eyes completely. When you see this resistance, it means you may want to retreat to something a little easier. Ask the group members to share something they did over the weekend with the person next to them. Have them do a breathing exercise on their own. Take it to a place that's a little easier so they can start to build a little "I can do this" trust with themselves and the workshop.

TAKE DIFFERENT LEARNING STYLES INTO ACCOUNT

Another thing to consider is different styles of learning. Everyone has different aptitudes for taking in information in different ways. We are all some combination of visual (sight-based), auditory (sound-based), kinesthetic (movement-based), and tactile (touch-based) learners. Each of us has one or two learning styles that are dominant in us. As a director or facilitator of a group, you can be more effective with the Creative Formula by touching on more than one of these styles, if not all of them, in any given session.

For example, if you are working through a new piece of music with your quartet, it might be beneficial to discuss important areas you'd like to hit before you begin (engaging auditory learners). Then you might follow by playing all the way through the piece without stopping (hitting kinesthetic, tactile, and auditory learners). Afterward, you could ask them to jot down any thoughts about the work and any areas they have questions on (visual and tactile learners). Follow it up with answering those questions and drawing on a whiteboard to emphasize points, or even simply describing the point you are making using visual imagery in your language (visual learners). Finally, you could have the group go through the motions of some piece of technique you are hoping to impart, repeating it several times (kinesthetic learners).

The result to this multimodal approach is that you will keep the group enthusiastic and engaged—in other words, in alignment. You will give them ample opportunities to allow through conversation, discussion, and jotting down ideas. You will also provide multiple ways that they can articulate, processing and formulating the entire work-through of the piece into something meaningful and clear.

In addition to informing how you might be most effective in groups, these learning styles can also relate to your own experience with the Creative Formula. They can point to where you might have the most strength and provide ideas for how you could incorporate new tactics to assist you in those areas that you don't. Say you are a choreographer who has an easy time with allowing. Once you are in the allowing frame of mind, you could spend the day there, playing and dreaming up tons of ideas. But it's the getting in there that's the hard part. You have trouble with alignment. If you know that you are an auditory as well as a kinesthetic learner (which, if you are a dancer, you very likely are), then you might try listening to a CD of the music (an effective activity for auditory learners) on your way to the studio in order to get into alignment.

Being an Allowing Leader

It sounds like a no-brainer, but I've seen this happen too many times not to bring it up. How many times have I sat in an improv workshop where the emphasis is on saying "Yes, and..." with an instructor who will interrupt mid-scene and shout out "NOOOOO!"

We can't instruct on a new paradigm while modeling the old one. When you are asking people to allow and say yes, be careful about how you are facilitating the process. Try to find ways to say "Yes, and..." to them as you guide them, rather than "No, that's not right." Be aware of this, because it's easy to be quick to correct people. Often it's what we ourselves as teachers have observed in other teachers, so it can be a tricky thing to avoid. Model what you are asking them to do in your facilitation, and the work will flow much more smoothly.

Don't say no to get them to say yes.

Your ideas for working with them should be as vast, diverse, flexible, and creative as you are asking them to be. Being present and able to pivot or shift the activity or energy in the room at any moment is key. Encourage them to hang in there. There is no rush to the Allowing process, and when you're in a group there can be a tendency to feel like others are getting there and you aren't. Extra encouragement that wherever they are is fine may be necessary. Help them understand that if they continue to dig and play, then eventually the need to articulate something will become clear. It's like finding your voice —at first you may need to clear your throat.

Articulation and Collaboration in a Group

Whenever you are creating a piece on a group, whether you are a choreographer making dance on a group of dancers, a composer creating parts for instrumentation, or a director developing the characters on a group of actors, the clearer you are about your variables, the more you open yourself up to the possibility of an exchange of ideas. When you are clear on the weird little rules of your universe, you give the others you're working with a clear realm to play within. Believe it or not, setting up a framework by doing a lot of the articulation work ahead of time gives way to more opportunity for group participation in the creative process. It's like setting up a scene. If people understand who they are playing and their relationship to one another, then you can say "Go!" and watch them explore the possibilities of the scenarios that unfold. If they are unclear on the weird little rules of your universe, then there are too many options and there will be a prevailing sense of uncertainty about whether they are doing it "right." You will waste time and lose trust.

I suggest that when working on people, you do not leave the articulation—the rules of the game you are playing—up to the group. The director, choreographer, or composer needs to carve out the roles and most of the movement vocabulary. Clarify and help steer and define those variables. With clearly defined variables, a group can move a piece forward brilliantly through allowing, which then serves as great feedback for further articulation. But ultimately, there should be one chef deciding what the menu is going to be and making the final call.

Working with Groups
Self-Assessment Questions

- ✓ Do people seem engaged?

- ✓ Am I giving them enough time to move from one step to another? (For example, are they aligned before we move on to allowing?)

- ✓ Do people seem to understand what they are supposed to be doing?

- ✓ Are people working together or avoiding each other?

- ✓ Am I utilizing different styles of learning?

- ✓ Is there good circulation in the group among participants?

- ✓ Am I staying observant and open to the needs and creative momentum of the group?

- ✓ Am I excited and interested in what the group is doing?

THE CREATIVE FORMULA
IN COACHING SESSIONS

W henever I'm asked how I work with people in coaching sessions, I give the analogy of untying a shoelace. Imagine a shoelace that is tied bunny-ears style in a simple bow knot. Now imagine that instead of having two ends coming out of the knot beneath the bunny-ear loops, there are several ends coming out, but there is only one that actually connects to the knot itself. When coaching people, I listen, I wait, I call them toward what they want—but mostly I wait for that loose end to reveal itself. If I tug on one loose end ever so gently and it easily unravels, the whole knot needs to be addressed before the entire project comes undone.

Coaching is like that. It really is that simple in some ways. I don't look at people as big complex knotted-up messes like a tangle of Christmas lights! They may want me to. And often, they'll tell me a story as though they are, but I never believe them. That's the biggest service I do.

Understanding and recognizing the three phases of the Creative Formula helps me recognize where my client stands. Once I began to articulate this framework, it has given me quick, accessible clarity to know what they might need—to get some movement and jostle their knots free, or just to try something different that might help them.

It isn't always directly coming from my analytical mind. Rather, I'll feel the energy of each of these steps. Alignment by itself feels calm and has a soothing stillness to it, like a clear pool. I can hear it in their deep breaths before the beginnings of thoughtful sentences. I can see it in their nodding heads and unwavering eyes.

Allowing, on the other hand, fills the room with excitement, and I can often spot it in wide eyes, eyebrows raised in epiphany, and openmouthed smiles. Physical gestures when someone is experiencing Allowing literally get bigger, taking up more space than before.

Articulation has a palpable, almost mathematical focus to it, and feels heavier than Allowing, but deeper too. I can see it in narrowed or darting eyes, hands coming together, and the presence of lots of wordy detail.

I can feel when the different ingredients are present or more dominant and when they're not. They are touchstones to doing effective and consistent work with the performers and creators that I work with.

Any coaching process is an in-depth and involved process, but it will prove helpful to show some of the ways in which the use of the Creative Formula can inform a coaching process. Here are some of my keys for unlocking someone, and my rules to live by for working with people one on one:

1. The Ultimate Goal Is Alignment

If I had to say that I focus on one thing throughout a coaching session, it would be the clarity of the person I'm working with. If they are confused or muddled, then I'm trying to discover what are they clear about, what can they get behind, and where their alignment is. As a coach, my job is to see clarity before they do, so I'm looking for it constantly. Often, it's easier for me to see it than it is for them, because they see all the details of the confusion and are mired in all the reasons they aren't clear. It's my job to find the clarity and focus on that before everything else.

II. LISTEN BEYOND THEIR WORDS

What often happens when I first start working with someone is that they want to tell me their story and all the reasons why they aren't getting anything done/feeling good onstage/able to create new work. But I've found it does absolutely no good to get involved in every detail. They know every detail intimately, which is why things are not working out for them! They are too close to the problem. I serve them by not buying into the problem. That is not to say that I don't empathize, that I don't listen compassionately, or that I don't hear what they're saying. I listen very, very deeply. But mostly, in the beginning, I'm listening to the plea underneath the words. I'm listening for their yearning. I do want to know what's going on with them, but I make sure I listen more to how their body is humming with their words, discordant or in agreement. Where are they contracted? How do I feel when I watch them speak? What words are they saying over and over again? Which ones are charged? What does their body seem to be reaching for? What is in the room with us that isn't being said? And then when we touch on those things, those new, helpful pieces wanting to come forward, we expand on them.

My philosophy is that people are capable of finding their own answers, so I relieve myself from the duty to sort it out. I empower them to realize the solution. If they've got me drudging through the nitty-gritty details of this and that, then in some ways they are staying stuck in the same energy of their problems.

III. DON'T LET THEM DEPEND ON YOUR APPROVAL

Remember? "I never trust anyone who doesn't trust me to trust myself."

The coaching process itself is as creative as making a piece of choreography or composing an aria. You are the director of an experience. The client has momentarily lost their ability to direct themselves. You are filling in as a surrogate until they can feel their feet on the ground and get some traction again to take off. The more you use the Creative Formula, the more you will come to be able to feel for what needs to come forward. You'll know when to push them, back off, or redirect. The ultimate goal is that they seek the solutions from inside. It's approaching the coaching work as a shaman, rather than as a drill sergeant. You are guiding a journey, not demanding they follow yours.

So, what does that really look like? You speak less and ask more questions. You don't assume what their problem is or what the answer is. You mirror what they say. If you think you see a solution or a gem of wisdom, then you repeat what they just said. Be wary of giving them your straight opinion. Share preferences if they ask, but not aesthetic judgments.

IV. Strategies to Allow New Possibilities

If you're enjoying this approach to coaching and have decided that you aren't into handing people prepackaged solutions, then how can you help them allow for new possibilities? Here are some of my strategies:

Borrow Happiness: If they are stuck in one area of their life, one thing you can do is to borrow from another area of their life where they are doing well. Do they have hobbies that come easily to them? Are they great at their job, but stuck in their art? Find a way to use the ease in one area of their life to help the place where they are stuck. If you are working with someone who is an amazing third-grade teacher but feels at a loss when it comes to creating their choreography, find out what makes it easy for them to be a creative teacher so that they might be able to transfer that to their work in the studio.

Act It Out: If they're fearful of a certain situation or an event that happened, act it out with them and see if you can help them make a different choice. In coaching sessions, they have the benefit of repetition. There is no pressure to get it right the first time. If you act something out with them and it doesn't go as they would like, then you can rewind to the place it took an uncomfortable turn and try something new. You can do this as many times as necessary. The experience of actually going through the motions and playing the game has the same effect as if it really happened. This process can move people forward exponentially by carving new emotional pathways.

Empowering Language: We can change our relationship to something simply by changing the way we speak about it. In what ways can you help them rename things in a more empowering way? Are there things that they feel very certain and confident about that you can borrow words from? Say that someone routinely refers to themselves as a "typical crazy artist." Is there a way they can reframe these qualities into something positive? Maybe they are "prolific with ideas" or "passionate about their work" instead.

Somatic Exercises: The physical body is a powerful tool for shifting the emotional body and serves as a resource to map out creative pathways. If you are working with someone and you've ended the session on a high note, have them create a simple movement encapsulating how they feel that they can repeat later. This will ground the emotional and mental work you do into the physical body and make it longer lasting and easier to return to.

Stay Compassionate: Coaching can sometimes be messy and dramatic work. In the beginning of working with someone, I typically spend 50 percent of the time listening to them cry. Most of us simply don't have a safe place to do that and so it comes out in coaching. It's fine. I don't make a big deal of it or coddle them, but I also bring as much love and compassion as I can. Compassion breeds trust. And with trust, anything is possible. This means staying open to what's coming up for them without judging them in any way or allowing it to trigger any experiences that you, as a coach, have had before. The more you are able to let them be OK and accept them, no matter what is coming up, then the more they will trust you and feel able to move past whatever they're going through.

V. ARTICULATION OF THE NEW STORY

The Return of the Old Story: There is often a moment, right before a big breakthrough, when someone wants to retell me their story. They feel the old misery slipping away and the ego wants to grab hold of it. They come to me and insist they are flawed; they tell the story they first told me, only more adamantly than before. They feel like they are having a breakdown, but really they're on the verge of a breakthrough. Be careful of what you articulate. Don't be their therapist. You are not there to dig up their past—too much. Sometimes it comes up, but I would suggest treading lightly in the details. Specificity breeds strong emotion, so be careful what you dig into details about, especially if you aren't trained in therapeutic work.

Ask Them to Make a Decision: There is a point at which you must ask them to make a choice to tell a new story, to take a stand for themselves in a new way. Jesse Koren and Sharla Jacobs articulate it so beautifully in their book *The Art of Attracting Clients*: "Because when you don't ask, the answer is always 'No.' When you do ask, you give people the opportunity to say 'Yes' to what their heart is calling them to say Yes to." The same principle applies when coaching someone, and the operative word is *ask*. Give them the option. This is consistent with your role as temporary leader. Ask them for it. Empower them to make a new choice for themselves when they're ready.

The more you practice the Creative Formula, the more you'll be able to use it yourself as you work with someone. Listening for the trail of interest, for what's a *yes*. Where is the movement headed? Is it beneficial? Are we judging or having preferences? Are we trying to jump to the conclusions (Articulation) too quickly? And you also feel for that crucial moment when you ask them to take a stand for themselves.

How I Know When My Work Is Done: There often comes a point near the end of working with someone where we have a session that's just soaring with energy. Ideas are flying around and there's much excitement about the new opportunities that have been opening up, whether in the unfolding of new work or in new projects or collaborations. I get swept up in the glee and creativity of my client and sometimes even make suggestions. This is awesome because they let me know they no longer need me by disregarding my ideas completely. This is when I know our work together, for this time, is coming to a close. They show me without a doubt that their trajectory and vision of themselves is the strongest in the room. I couldn't wish anything bigger for them than that.

Coaching
Self-Assessment Questions

✓ Am I putting my client's alignment and clarity as my main objective before trying to do anything else?

✓ Is there anything about their story that I'm buying into that doesn't serve them?

✓ Am I spending a lot of time listening to many specific details and finding myself trying to help them figure it all out? (This is an indication you might be buying into their story. It's imperative to pay attention to how you feel. If the details are starting to make you feel overwhelmed, exasperated, negative, or at a loss, then it's time to switch gears and try Alignment or Allowing.)

✓ How do I feel after coaching? Uplifted? Drained?

✓ Do I find myself giving my judgment or opinion about things too frequently with this person?

✓ Am I staying open to whatever comes up for them in sessions, or am I attached to their transformation, progress, or getting results?

THE CREATIVE FORMULA
ONSTAGE

Performance itself is a fleeting thing. We work for weeks, months, years to practice and get it just right and then we go out there onstage and...it goes how it goes. After that it's over and done and there's nothing we can do to change it. The pressure of this fact can be crippling. But it's also what makes being onstage wildly exciting and fun. For those of us who love performing, it becomes an addiction. The rush of that open space, that jumping-out-of-an-airplane feeling, is risky and glorious. You can plan and practice all you want, but in the end you never know exactly how it's going to go. When it goes great, you feel transported somehow, or almost superhumanly heroic. It makes you crave that experience and you're always looking for it every time afterwards. When it doesn't go as planned, and you aren't prepared to recover from that, it can be miserable and crushing. But there are definitely tools within the wisdom of the Creative Formula to help you create magic onstage and also navigate those emotions when you don't.

Just as we are creating in the studio, we are also creating every moment as it happens during a performance onstage. The only difference is that we are doing it in front of others. There's no chance to go back and do it again. The Creative Formula, and bringing an acute awareness of the three steps into the realm of performance, can really help to shape and refine this experience.

ALIGNMENT

Just as you might align before stepping into the studio to work, it's also important to align before a performance—maybe even more so, because in addition to needing to stay steady through your own critical thoughts, you are also going to need to be aligned enough to steer through the crowd of others: performers, crew members, the audience. The energy backstage before a show can be frenetic—I personally love it (it feels like we are getting ready for a party!)—but it can throw you off. Allowing yourself extra preparation time, warm-up time, and quiet space to balance your nerves is important.

When an artist goes onstage to perform, whether it is music, dance, or theatre, they are expected to show the audience something that's magical, just a little larger than life, or a little better. They are called upon to transport us into another world and perform wondrous feats of physical and mental acuity. It is no wonder then that many performers have special preparations, little rituals for themselves to put them in the optimum mind-set. On the flip side of this, I also think we can sometimes get a little too precious about how much we need before a show.

Personally, my best performances sometimes happen when I almost forget about the fact that I'm about to go onstage. I'm having fun getting ready with others in the show. I'm in a state of relaxed eagerness, of grounded excitement. Also, things tend to go best when I have as few conflicts or interactions with the production in my way as possible. This is where having a really outstanding crew is a precious commodity. My eyes actually tear up when I think of how on top of it and supportive the backstage professionals I've worked with have been over the years—I'm so grateful. Props where they need to be, lighting and music cues happening when they are supposed to; the crew members, by doing their jobs right, give me a sense of trust. I can just be in the magic instead of worrying about what's happening backstage. Those are the best performances.

ALLOWING AND ARTICULATION

Once you are onstage, Allowing and Articulation are happening simultaneously. If you are performing a choreographed, composed, or set piece, then you know what you are supposed to be doing onstage and so it would appear that the creative process is over with, but most of us can understand why this isn't the case. If the performance were so set in stone that it was the exact same every time, then it would be so boring that no one would ever go to see it. Truly. That's why the Creative Formula is relevant even up to and through the end of a performance. It's important to continue playing the game and dancing the dance between Allowing and Articulation even when you're onstage. Staying present to what is interesting to you, making choices in the moment, and looking for ways to be most clear are still vitally important during performance.

STAYING TRUE TO YOUR WEIRD LITTLE RULES

There is a thing that can sometimes happen onstage when the excitement of being in front of people triggers the show-stealing beast inside a performer and they break the rules of the universe that's been created onstage. Usually it's seen in amateurs, but surprisingly I've experienced it with professionals as well. There is nothing more infuriating than being onstage with someone who decides to change the rules on you all of a sudden. This is dangerous territory and can ruin a production. It's important that while you continue that game of Allowing and Articulation onstage, that you also play within the vocabulary and weird little rules that have already been defined in the rehearsal or preparation period. You worked to clarify those things for a reason, and having them should give you a whole wonderful world to play inside. There's no need to reach outside of that and upstage everyone else. To do so is to abandon your performing partners and make a waste of the energy that went into the creative process.

The Apologetic Performer and Why You Shouldn't Be One

It's happened to all of us at one time or another. The off night. Your performance doesn't match up to your high artistic standards. Afterwards, you find yourself apologizing to audience members, musicians, other performers. Well, you shouldn't. This is one of the biggest mistakes that performers make. I should know: I've done it myself.

I remember once when I performed at a well-known flamenco tablao gig in San Francisco and I sorta bombed. I accidentally catapulted the cane I was dancing with into the audience. Yes, really. It landed on someone's dinner table and bounced to the floor pitifully while I lumbered off the stage to retrieve it. To make matters worse, I believe I remember that a baby was sitting at the table with its family too. Talk about horrible moments! After that, I couldn't seem to recover and get back into the flow of the performance. Hey, it happens. It was such a bad night that I had to bite my tongue and grimace as I passed by people I knew at the bar on the way to the dressing room. Backstage, I groaned and moaned to my fellow musicians and the other dancer. But I regretted it later, mostly because no one cared. What I've always known, but learn more and more, is this:

Never apologize for simply being human and messing up onstage. The main reason is that it diminishes people's experience of your performance. There are many things that are not noticeable to most people, especially things like nervousness happening inside of you. Very keenly observant people who know you very well and see you perform often may notice when you have an off night, but you must remember two things:

1. Everyone is seeing you through the lens of their own experience.
2. Most people are just thinking about themselves most of time.

What we as performers provide has the potential to be a transportive, sensational, moving, magical experience. Through the act of performing, we are giving our art away as an experience that is received by the audience in whatever way they choose to view it. It is out of our control. When an audience member actually has the luck of finding you in the sea of adoring fans, or the courage to approach you to remark on your performance, the last thing they want to hear is a monologue from the insecure voice in your head. So learn to smile and take a compliment. It is an opportunity for your audience to be on the inside and share in your magical experience—even if, for you, it wasn't so magical.

There are a couple exceptions to the no-apologies rule. Apologize if you screw up in a way that seriously affects or throws off anyone onstage with you. (See previous section, re: show-stealing beast.) Hopefully, they are nice and say, "Oh well, don't worry about it." If they are really professional and you just made an honest mistake, then they might say, "No! That was awesome, oh my god that was my favorite part! Are you kidding? Did you see what I did after THAT?" They will understand the value of making everything right onstage and that true magic happens from the unexpected.

The other exception to the no-apologies rule is if you do something that physically endangers or harms your audience. Like throwing your cane at them. Then, yes. Apologize for that.

MAKE HOW YOU FEEL MATTER MOST

There is something beautiful about sharing your art onstage, allowing yourself to take up space with your talent and reveal the inner bits of your soul. But it should never be at the expense of your own alignment. I always tell the artists I work with to get a little selfish onstage. I know it sounds like a contradiction—get selfish to be generous—but unless you do get a little self-absorbed and allow your attention and love to be felt inside of yourself, then how else would you have anything of value to share? And on that note, how you feel about your performance should be your true barometer of how it went. Just use the audience as a backup in case you feel like you didn't do so hot.

By this I mean, when you are onstage and allowing, you want your trail of interest and your focus to be lighting up with fun. If you can manage to keep that focus, then you'll feel great when you walk offstage. It's also very likely that the audience loved it too. Bully for them. But in those times when you struggled to keep your focus, when you let negative thoughts creep in, felt like you were just going through the motions, or had a complete mess-up onstage, then it is helpful to have the reflection of the audience. It is likely it wasn't as bad as you felt it was. It is also likely that no one saw you mess up. You have to remember that people bring themselves to the experience when they are watching you. They are seeing you through their own lens and there is nothing you can do to control that. So, in those times when you feel low about what just went down, if there is an audience member telling you that they loved it, I recommend listening to them talk about it. Let their impression reach you, sink in, and become the new version in your mind.

YOUR MASTERPIECE

The fragrance of the apple tree in your backyard has been calling to you all morning long, floating over the grass and into your face through the open kitchen window. It's a sunny morning in September. Although it is warming up quickly, there's a distinct crispness to the cool air, signaling that moment when it feels like summer is holding a note just a little too long before giving over center stage to fall. You decide to bake one of your apple pies, your specialty, for the small dinner party you're having tonight. You grab a colander and head out across the grass towards the tree.

Everything about this process of making a pie pleases you. You take your time picking just the right apples, relishing the firm feel of them in your hands, the warmth of the sunshine on your hair as you stand out there, sniffing, selecting just the perfect ripe ones. In your kitchen, your fingers dance through the spices in the cupboard, the combination a little different each time, and for this one you find yourself reaching for the cardamom. The amount you are adding will hardly be recognizable, but it's an excuse to open the jar and deeply inhale the scent, bringing back memories of sipping chai tea on your world travels to India, the Middle East, Greece. Each pie you make is a little different, but the mixture for the crust is a science and you relish the measuring out of the flour and the sugar just so—using a butter knife to drag across the top of the cup, evening out the amount neatly. You slice the crisp apples and place them in a pinwheel inside the crust. Today, you are feeling a little fancy and so you find yourself pulling out your grandmother's ancient serving bowl to place the baked pie in after it cools, the luscious green leaves in the design curling over the edges and mirroring the pie crust pattern just inside.

Your friends all look forward to your pies. By now, they practically expect them. Tonight is no exception, and yet something about this evening is different. The pie is more than just the centerpiece of conversation at the dinner party. After a few bites, everyone at the table seems to slow down just a touch, savoring the unique flavor of this special pie. The chitter-chatter of the separate conversations slows to a halt. Simply and easily, people begin sharing stories from their lives, one by one, in a relaxed manner, with the entire table. Every so often, there is silence, only the sound of bites being taken, a sip of a drink, the nearly imperceptible sounds of pleasure. For years to come, everyone will remember that night and the feelings they shared together at your table. That pie that you baked so easily and with such delight will be remembered. Whenever they run into you, they'll all mention it using the same two distinct words.

Your masterpiece.

Join Me in the Lab!

Congratulations on reading this book and taking this step towards partnership with your muse! The more you listen, the more you will hear, beloved Artist. I welcome you to continue your creative journey with me and join me in the lab by visiting www.PerformersandCreatorsLab.com. Sign up for my free email list, and you will get access to the latest work and discoveries from me and others who choose to join me there. The work is never done, and by joining us you'll have access to the newest video content, tips, tools, meditations, and findings about the creative leading edge.

With all of my heart, I encourage you to continue to create your original work and totally kill it onstage. You, lovely one, are tasked with the creating of stuff and imagining new ways, remember? It's an important job, because if you can't imagine something different, then who else will? Your work is waiting.

BIG LOVE,

Holly

ACKNOWLEDGMENTS

Having spent most of my life as a performer, I'm a bit of a cowboy when it comes to the creative process and have grown used to, accepted, and now relish the ephemeral nature of a live dance or theatre performance. You work to make something as clean as possible for weeks in the studio, usually alone, but then once you perform it...show's over, folks. What's done is done. It's over and there's no going back to perfect it. It's taken me years to sink in and enjoy that aspect of it, only to now start writing books. Books: where there is something of substance, taking up space, that lasts more than a mere moment and is expected to be polished. I would not have made it through the tedium of finishing this book without the help of my patient editor, Norah Sarsour, and my hero in the final hour, Harlow Carpenter. A huge thank-you to them for sorting through the shit nuggets. I would also like to thank all past, present, and future clients, the artists who are my inspiration for this sacred work. And finally, I would like to thank my son, Aleister, my little pink tornado who has been my biggest teacher. You came into the world with the heart of a Buddha and the irreverence of puppy and at once, I knew you were mine.

INFLUENTIAL BOOKS
AND ADDITIONAL RESOURCES

Ball, William. *A Sense of Direction: Some Observations on the Art of Directing*. Hollywood: Drama Publishers/Quite Specific Media, 1984.

Bogart, Anne, and Tina Landau. *The Viewpoints Book: A Practical Guide to Viewpoints and Composition*. New York: Theatre Communications Group, 2005.

Cameron, Julia. *The Artist's Way: A Spiritual Path to Higher Creativity*. New York: Penguin Putnam, 1992.

Christensen, Tanner. *The Creativity Challenge: Design, Experiment, Test, Innovate, Build Create, Inspire, and Unleash Your Genius*. Avon, MA: Adams Media, 2015.

Fey, Tina. *Bossypants*. New York: Little, Brown and Company, 2011.

Halprin, Daria. *The Expressive Body in Life, Art and Therapy: Working with Movement, Metaphor and Meaning*. London: Jessica Kingsley Publishers, 2003.

Hicks, Esther, and Jerry Hicks. *Ask and It Is Given: Learning to Manifest Your Desires*. Carlsbad, CA: Hay House, 2004.

Jennings, Simon. *The Complete Artist's Manual: The Definitive Guide to Painting and Drawing*. San Francisco: Chronicle Books, 2013.

Koren, Jesse, and Sharla Jacobs. *The Art of Attracting Clients*. Santa Cruz: Thrive Academy, 2008.

Smith-Autard, Jacqueline. *Dance Composition: A Practical Guide to Creative Success in Dance Making.* New York: Bloomsbury Methuen Drama, 2013.

Tharp, Twyla. *The Creative Habit: Learn It and Use It for Life.* New York: Simon & Schuster, 2003.

ABOUT THE AUTHOR

Holly Shaw is a leading expert in creativity and performance owing to her thirty year career performing on TV, in film, and on stages all over the world, combined with her experience as a hypno and somatic therapist, creativity researcher and coach. Shaw facilitates workshops in performance and creative composition, is a sought after speaker, and coaches all kinds of performing artists, from Grammy-nominated singers to world-class dancers, in the San  Francisco Bay Area where she lives as well as New York, L.A., and internationally. Find out more at PerformersandCreatorsLab.com

Made in the USA
Monee, IL
26 November 2019